A COAL CAMP CHRONICLE:

Rememberin' My Raisin'

By

Trula Vandell Gray
With John Vandell

International Standard Book Number 0-87012-804-3
Library of Congress Control Number 2011900580
Printed in the United States of America
Copyright © 2011 by Trula Gray
Lillington, NC
All Rights Reserved
2011

McClain Printing Company
Parsons, WV
www.mcclainprinting.com
2011

PROLOGUE

The coalfields of southern West Virginia were opened to the outside world in the late 1880's with the building of the Coaldale Tunnel on the Norfolk and Western Railroad, near Maybeury, West Virginia. This tunnel allowed access to southern West Virginia's timber and coal resources, and the railroad was the main mode of transportation for the rugged area for many years.

Hemphill is one of many coal camps located in McDowell County, West Virginia's southernmost county. It is like most other coal camps in that the houses were built by the coal companies and were separated into groups determined by a man's job in the mines—small basic houses with no plumbing for laborers, larger houses with plumbing for bosses or other salaried employees, with the largest, fanciest house for the mine superintendent. The residents also lived in certain areas of the coal camp, according to their ethnicity, with African American or Italian miners occupying only certain sections of the coal camp. There were company stores, carpenter shops, fire houses, churches, beer joints, and, of course, a post office.

Hemphill was like most West Virginia coal camps in many ways, but it was also a unique community. Most coal camps were owned and controlled by one coal company. Hemphill was actually composed of three camps that lined the Tug River just about one mile from Welch, the county seat. The mines in Warwick Hollow and Orkney Hollow were owned by the New River Pocahontas Coal Company, and the Shaft Bottom camp was owned by the Kingston Pocahontas Coal Company (later known as the Semet Solvay Coal Company.) The coal companies owned the land, the houses, the roads, and the stores. As long as the mines were open, miners paid a few dollars rent each month, and the properties were painted, repaired, and otherwise maintained by the coal companies.

  Most houses in Hemphill were wooden structures built around 1920, but by 1960 the three mines in Hemphill had "shut down", mainly due to mechanization of the mines and high cost of coal production. When the mines closed, the houses were sold to individuals at very reasonable prices, usually about five hundred dollars per room. Some shrewd businessmen bought several houses and resold them at a profit. With maintenance in the hands of individual owners, some of the houses became untidy, even dirty, while others were maintained immaculately. When the coal companies relinquished ownership of their Hemphill properties, the Orkney Hollow area became the area for Welch's trash dump, a popular place for townsfolk from Welch to come for target practice, shooting at the many rats inhabiting the dump. This added to Hemphill's less than desirable reputation as a residential area.

To understand how things in McDowell County (and Hemphill), West Virginia, might appear to outsiders, this story is told of a young teacher who first arrived in Welch in the late 1930's:

I got on the passenger train in Bluefield. As the train left the station, it began a downhill descent and continued downhill until it stopped in Welch. Along the way, beside the railroad tracks arch-shaped brick coke ovens were belching smoke, flames, and fumes, as they heated raw coal into a charcoal-like substance called "coke". I felt as if I had truly descended into hell.

The events described in this book are true, based on family recollections and retellings. Even though the events really occurred, they did not all happen during the actual years mentioned in the story. Some names have been changed.

With love and gratitude, this book is dedicated to the memory of my parents, Sis and Lacy. I owe special thanks to my brother Ron for the maps, to my sister for help in editing, and, of course, to John, who coaxed me into writing our story.

Hemphill, West Virginia

Easter 1960

CHAPTER 1

"Randy Cochran's back! Randy Cochran's back!" The words both chilled and confused me as my brother John ran toward me shouting the news. It was my job that day to go to Stafford's Grocery, the "jottem-down store", to buy a short loaf of "light" bread for Mom. As I heard John's terrifying news, I clutched the thirty cents that Mom had entrusted to me for the purchase and kept my eyes peeled for the dreaded Randy Cochran.

I had never met, or even seen Randy, but his reputation was part of Hemphill legend and lore. We never really knew why he was sent to Pruntytown (the West Virginia Industrial Home for Boys—a.k.a. REFORM

SCHOOL); but we knew that whatever he did to be sent there, he kept doing it over and over because he left and returned to Hemphill every year or two.

 As I rounded "the curve" (called that because it was such a sharp turn in the one-lane road that cars had to blow their horns to warn oncoming drivers of their presence), I could see the church steps. From the steep rock steps I could see Randy Cochran's house, as well as most of Hemphill. The Cochran house was like most of the four-room, gray or white wooden houses with paint peeling and dirt yards in the coal camp called Hemphill. It hung precariously on the side of the hill in Orkney Holler, one of the three "hollers" (deep valleys) that made up the conglomerate community of Hemphill, West Virginia. Randy's house looked no different from the neighboring houses, but it seemed to stand out with an air of mystery, at least to my fearful eyes. I imagined a dark haired, beady-eyed, smudge-faced boy with an evil grin, watching my every move.

 There was no sign of the infamous Randy as I headed down the twenty-five stone steps, which had normal steps and deep steps that took two strides to navigate. The large sandstones in the steps were bound together with cement, and there were two-foot walls on both sides. At the bottom of the church steps I quickly passed one of the few brick structures in Hemphill, the Hemphill Methodist Church, newly built around 1957. Across a dirt curved road near the church was my destination, Stafford's Grocery. I cautiously approached and opened the rusty screen door, still watching for Randy as I entered.

    Stafford's (called "the jottem down store" by Dad because they jotted down what you needed on a slip of paper) was owned by Frank Stafford and his grandmotherly wife. They lived in an apartment above the store, and Frank made furniture, like the beautiful trundle bed they showed my parents and me the one time we were invited to visit the apartment. Stafford's sold the everyday essentials for life in Hemphill: bread, milk, Orange Crush, Grape Nehi, penny candy, and such. But, the greatest attraction for kids was the gumball machine.

    If you put a penny in the machine, you could get sweet, juicy gum, whose flavor lasted about thirty seconds. Or, you could get a "speckled ball", redeemable for a Mr. Goodbar, valued at five cents. It was our first experience with gambling, and we took every opportunity to spend a penny to get a nickel's worth of chocolate. Although I put many pennies in the machine, I remember winning the candy bar only once.

    On this March day I had no penny for the gumball machine. So, I asked Mrs. Stafford for a short loaf of "light" bread (what we called white bread), gave her the thirty cents and left. Clutching the brown paper bag with the cellophane wrapped Sunbeam bread in it, I walked along the main road, around the wooden store building, toward home on Spruce Street. There was no sign of Randy as I walked back up the stone church steps, around the curve, down the paved road to house number 135. What a relief!

As I entered the back door, the smell of pinto beans greeted my nostrils, and the clattering of the lid as the pot boiled was a familiar sound to my cold ears—too familiar these days.

"Beans again?" I complained. It seemed that we had "brown beans" seasoned with a chunk of fatback every other day.

"Just think of them as coal miners' strawberries," Mom answered without reprimanding me for whining. "That's what my father used to call them back during the Depression."

"You made a quick trip to Stafford's", said Mom, as she poured the cornbread batter into the melted grease in the iron skillet. I didn't answer until the batter had stopped sizzling and the skillet was in the oven.

"It is cold outside; so I ran part of the way," I lied. I didn't want to admit that fear of a boy I didn't even know had quickened my step.

March, 1960, was like any other March in the coalfields of West Virginia. Dreary days were interrupted by a few sunny ones scattered here and there. The threat of snow was always there, but the roadsides, gullies, and hillsides still had dirty remnant of bygone snowfalls that had melted and refrozen and melted and refrozen many times that winter. Though, technically, spring would arrive in March, the sunny days were deceiving, allowing blustery winds to bite noses and tops of ears and to scrub cheeks until they were rough and red.

  March was the month of family birthdays—my sister Janice was born on March 7, 1943, and my younger brother John was born on March 8, 1954. Janice always had a home-made red velvet cake and presents for her birthday, and John always had the leftover half of the cake for his birthday. He did, however, have his own present. In 1960, it was a box of matchbox cars that he could spend hours playing with his friend Larry. John and Larry would build roads in the dirt around the roots of the big maple tree in Larry's back yard, but it was still too cold for that in early March. We usually still had to wear coats, gloves, and scarves (hats for boys) until April or May.

  April in Hemphill was always an exciting month. April 1 was not only April Fool's Day when Dad would always say, "Your shoe's untied—April Fool", but it was also John L. Lewis's Birthday. John L. Lewis was instrumental in unionizing the coal workers during the 1940's, and his birthday was celebrated every year with a holiday for coal miners. More adventurous for our family was the fact that Dad usually traded cars on that day. The new pink and black Dodge that he brought home on April 1, 1960, caused an argument with Mom, as did each new car he would bring home. She would pout for a week or so and then realize that is the way things would always be on April 1. After the initial "pouting spell" Mom always said, "We might go to the poor house, but we will go there in a new car."

Easter came on April 17, 1960, but we spent weeks preparing for the event. The first sign that Easter was on the way was the pungent odor of vinegar, beet juice (from pickled beets that Mom had canned last September) and spices. When we smelled that distinctive smell, we knew that Mom was making pickled eggs. She would boil at least three dozen eggs, put them in gallon jars, and pour the hot beet juice/vinegar/spice mixture over the warm eggs. Dad insisted that the eggs be allowed to "pickle" for two weeks; so, we dared not taste them until the beet juice had penetrated its pinkish-purplish color through each egg into the yolk. These tart purple eggs would be a special treat for Easter dinner and many days thereafter.

A goodly portion of the first payday in April would be spent for "Easter outfits" for us kids. I always got a navy blue duster (a lightweight coat), white gloves and anklets (socks), patent leather shoes with buckled straps (which no one would dare wear before Easter), a dress with a crinoline slip that made the sound of crumpling paper when I walked, and, of course, an Easter bonnet. My younger brother John always got a new shirt, a suit, and shoes. Mom rarely got a new Easter frock because of lack of money, and Dad didn't go to the Easter services at church; so he didn't need "Sunday-go-to-meetin' clothes". We would usually go to Penney's or Cox's Department Store in Welch and try on clothes until we found something that fit. It was not hard for John to shop, but according to the clerks, I was "big boned"; so it was harder for me to find a nice outfit. Little did I know that "big boned" is a synonym for "chubby".

    After shopping for clothes, we would always go to G. C. Murphy's and look at the live Easter chicks and ducklings. You could hear them and smell them as you got closer to them in the basement section of the store. The chicks were brightly colored—red, green, blue, purple (my favorite). I think they dyed them in the shell before they hatched. The ducks remained their natural yellow color.

    During the week between Palm Sunday and Easter, it was my job to take my younger brother John to Angelo's Barber Shop for his Easter haircut. Carefully clutching the dollar that Mom gave me (I rarely had paper money), I took John's hand and walked silently up Spruce Street's one lane that followed the bank of Tug River, until we came to the blind curve, past the stone "church steps", and up the hill to the two-lane "county road", where the red, white and blue twirling stripes of the barber pole marked our destination. Timidly, I entered with John following close behind. "Well, here is John, with his 'little mommy'", shouted Angelo, as he and a burly customer laughed. We sat in the red vinyl chairs with chrome frames that lined one wall, while Angelo, with his dark, slick hair and wire rimmed glasses, clipped and talked, clipped and talked to the man in the chair. Italian opera music played softly in the background. The customer was telling a joke about a traveling salesman, and when I became interested, he suddenly began speaking Italian. Then, he and Angelo laughed big belly laughs, but John and I failed to see what was so funny. Angelo continued to talk to the customer as he clipped, saying, "The first time I gave John a haircut, I thought he was so pretty that I just had to kiss him." Well, that embarrassed John, but the customer seemed to understand.

 Finally, it was John's turn for his Easter haircut. He climbed up into the big black vinyl chair. This time there was more clipping than talking, especially since John wasn't in any mood to answer Angelo's questions. There was no Italian spoken while John was in the chair.

 As the haircut got to its final stage, Angelo pulled out the electric clippers and buzzed them along John's neckline. Then, he picked up the tall clear bottle with green liquid, poured some in his hand, and put it on John's freshly cut hair. I thought it must have been Wildroot Hair Tonic, since the sign on the wall advertised Wildroot, with a picture of a man with slick shiny hair like the movie star Clark Gable's hair. The smell was pungent and manly, and we could always tell when a man or boy had just visited Angelo. As John jumped down from the chair, I shyly handed Angelo the dollar and said, "Thank you." We then silently left, but not before Angelo gave each of us his traditional treat, a stick of Juicy Fruit Gum. Then, we walked silently home. When we got home, Mom said in a relieved voice, "I am so glad Angelo didn't give John that G.I. haircut like he did last Easter. That took four months to grow out. Angelo always gives boys the kind of haircut HE wants them to have."

The Saturday before Easter Mom, my older sister Janice, and I visited Myrtle's Beauty Salon in Welch for our yearly "permanent". Myrtle attended our church, and her shop was located in the same building as the Trailways bus terminal. If you had to go to the bathroom during your visit to Myrtle's, you stepped out the back screen door, directly into the bus station's waiting area, past the counter with the glass tanks pumping lemonade and orangeade down the sides. We could only look at the tanks and wish because Mom had to be "tight" to afford Easter clothes, etc.

Myrtle's Beauty Shop was a store-front utilitarian establishment with one wall lined with mirrors and counters where the beauticians (usually two or three) worked. Two other walls were lined with large brown vinyl chairs, topped by barrel-shaped, hot, noisy hair drying machines that resembled oversized helmets.

The torturous session usually began with waiting while Myrtle began to work on Mom's hair: shampooing, cutting, and pin curling with small plastic curlers fastened by black rubber straps. I looked at the dated Life magazines while I waited. I didn't care because it was a treat to look at ANY magazine.

Finally, it would be my turn. Washing and cutting weren't so bad, though I was too short to lean comfortably over the large sink. This caused a pain in my neck, and the shampoo often ended up in my eyes. Even the rolling up was not so bad, although it seemed to take forever as I tried to sit still in the big chair and look in the mirror while Myrtle carefully put each strand in metal clips and the small plastic curlers. Next came the application of the permanent wave solution. The stench burned my nose as the liquid burned my scalp. I waited for a time with the putrid concoction on my hair, dripping onto my forehead, necessitating the use of the towel that was draped on my neck. Then it was rinsed out, and something called neutralizer was put on my hair with the curlers still in. Then, long strips of cotton were pulled from a blue paper wrapper and placed around my hairline and over each ear. This entire masterpiece was covered with a heavy triangular shaped net that was tied at the nape of the neck. The process would take more than an hour, and then the ultimate torture would begin.

Being placed under the hair dryer meant sitting still for what seemed like hours. The clips and curlers got hot. My ears and scalp got hot. If the cotton was supposed to protect my ears, it wasn't working. Putting my hands over my ears didn't help either. It only made my hands hot. The dryer was so loud that I couldn't hear anything, not even the "all aboard" announcement for the bus to Hemphill, Capels, and Davy. The announcer always said in a monotone voice, "Havaco, Wilco, anywhere you wanna go." The dryer was so loud and hot that even the Life Magazine could not pacify me, and I whined, "Is it dry yet?" Everyone acted as if they could not hear me.
	I tried to take my mind off the burning sensation by imagining bus trips, but I had only ridden the bus from the station in Welch with Mom to Hemphill. When we neared Spruce Street, Mom would reach above the window and pull a cord that extended from the front to the back of the bus. Then the driver knew to stop at the end of Spruce Street, and we could walk the rest of the way home.
	Finally, after what seemed like hours a kind beautician turned off the infernal machine. I sat long enough for the clips and curlers to cool, and finally, the new coiffure was unveiled. It was awful—blunt bangs, much too short, with frizzy curls and the smell of the residue of the solutions. However, I really didn't care because I just wanted the ordeal to be over. When it came time for Mom

to pay Myrtle for the three new hairstyles for Mom, my sister, and me, Myrtle just waved her hand and said, "I'll see you at church." I guess Myrtle knew about "tight times."

    Since Easter Sunday, 1960, was in April, it was one of the few Easter Sundays that we could wear our new finery without a winter coat. When John and I awoke that sunny morning, we found our Easter baskets filled with malted milk eggs, unwrapped jelly beans and big pastel-colored, sugary eggs with white nougat in the middle nestled in the green Easter grass in bottom of the basket, marshmallow bunnies, and Peeps. We also found shoe boxes with holes in the lids. Inside mine was a purple chick, and inside John's was a yellow duckling. We were elated. They were so cute and fuzzy. John was so excited he ran outside in his pajamas, carrying his shoebox of duckling. Our black and white cat, Sylvester, was on the back porch in front of the door. Forgetting a cardinal household rule (NEVER pick up Sylvester), John tried to gently lift the cat out of his way. Immediately, I heard screams from the porch. Sylvester had decorated both of John's bare arms with long bloody scratches. But John saved his precious duck from the cat, so far.

    The 1960 Easter Sunday service at the First Church of God was much like the services in the previous four years. We sang "The Old Rugged Cross" and "Up from the Grave He Arose", and the preacher preached about the Resurrection.

When we got home after church, we changed out of our "church clothes", enjoyed some Easter candy, had fried chicken and pickled eggs for dinner, and played with the chick and duckling. It was during Sunday dinner that Dad told the well-known story about Easter when he was a "young'un".

When I was a young'un, we didn't get candy at Easter—or any other time either. The Saturday before Easter, I went to the woods, found a shady place, and got me some moss. I took it home and lined a "warsh pan" with it. The next morning the Rabbit had come and laid colored eggs in the pan.

"What's a wash pan?" I asked, between bites of buttery roll.

"We didn't have a bathroom; so we carried water from the well, put it in a round porcelain coated metal pan and 'warshed' up on the back porch. So, I used that pan for the Rabbit to lay eggs in," Dad answered patiently.

After Easter Dinner, we had planned to hide the Easter eggs that we had dyed on Saturday afternoon, but, instead, Dad took John and me over to Uncle Buddy's and Aunt Anna Belle's house on the Warwick Holler side of Hemphill. Anna Belle had a huge basket of colored eggs, and some of them had coins taped on them. We walked down the dirt road on the hill over to the old Hemphill Clubhouse, which was in ruins by that time. It was just a stone foundation with a few piles of bricks lying around on a secluded hillside. It had once been a hub of social activity for Hemphill coal miners, a large stone and brick building where single coal miners "boarded" (slept and ate) and socialized.

    At the site of the old clubhouse, sprouting with weeds, we met Mom's Cousin Oscar's kids. I was a little afraid of Oscar's kids. I didn't know them, and they seemed to be dressed rather shabbily with crooked teeth and messy, even dirty, hair. The oldest boy, Junior, even had an overgrown Mohawk haircut left over from 1957. We all had a good time finding the eggs among the old stone walls and newly green weeds. It was especially exciting when I found a blue egg with a nickel taped to it.

    After the egg hunt, John and I walked home, and I told Mom about the kids with ugly hair, teeth, and clothes, and even uglier names. Mom said, "Trula, you're gettin' above your raisin'. You need to respect others, even if they don't have as much as you do. Oscar's kids depend on government commodities (flour, dried beans, dried eggs, and dried milk) delivered every month to unemployed people around here. And, when I was growing up in Hemphill my family didn't have anything either, not even 'commodities'. I remember one time during the Depression when my dad hopped a train to look for work and left us kids with my older sister Tootsie in charge. I think she was about fourteen at the time. He was gone a whole week, and all we had to eat was a gallon jar of blackberry jam that Aunt Ida had given us and biscuits that Tootsie made from lard and flour. Those were hard times, but even though I didn't have much, I still needed love and respect—just like Oscar's kids do."

As she spoke, I couldn't help but recall one of Mom's favorite sayings, "Pride goeth before a fall." I began to feel guilty about my judgments about Oscar's kids, but I was still glad that we didn't have to eat "commodities" all the time. Pinto beans were boring enough for me.

The week after Easter, the neighbor's dog killed John's Easter duckling. My purple chick survived, but as it outgrew the shoe box, Mom talked me into giving it to a neighbor. She took it to a relative who owned a farm. (At least that is what she told me.)

CHAPTER 2

The first week in May was the highlight of a Hemphill kid's life. It was the one time each year that the Carnival came to nearby Welch and set up the sideshows, games, and rides at Linkous Park. The rides were my favorite part, especially the Scrambler. If you could get a boy to ride it with you, it would sling the two of you together in a most scintillating way. I hated the Tilt-a-Whirl because the spinning and jerking would make me nauseous.

As usual, it rained almost every day of Carnival Week in 1960. The planners should have consulted my dad before scheduling the Carnival. He would have told them that the first week in May is when the blackberries bloom, and everyone knows that it rains a lot during that time (Blackberry Winter). However, John and I waited all week for a sunny Saturday afternoon to go to the Carnival. Mom and Janice had gone to Cincinnati on the train, and Dad was working at the Black Wolf Mine that Saturday. So, John and I were playing catch with a baseball in the back yard, killing time before we would walk to Welch and go to the Carnival that afternoon. John was throwing, and I was catching, if you could call it that. I was doing fairly well, chasing every other ball that I missed, until John threw a wild one, and it crashed into a window, cracking it from top to bottom.

We were really scared. Dad's mandates to the kids had always been "Don't touch anyone's car, and don't do damage to a house, especially ours." Since Dad had given us two dollars each to spend at the Carnival, we did the only thing that we thought might appease him. We did not go to the Carnival, and hoped that the four dollars would be used to replace the window.

That evening when Dad came home, he asked us about the Carnival. We reluctantly showed him the window. We were amazed that he did not get angry. In fact, he told us to get ready to go to the Carnival. Dad took us to the Sterling Drive-In. When the "curb girl" came to the car, Dad rolled down his window and ordered three foot- long hot dogs and three chocolate milkshakes, a very rare treat for us. When the curb girl returned, she hooked the metal tray to the slightly rolled up window, and Dad distributed the tissue-wrapped hot dogs with chili, mustard, and onions, and the chocolate milkshakes with the fat straws. After three sips, the paper straw collapsed, and we had to suck and suck until our cheeks hurt to get the thick milkshakes into our waiting mouths. We finally gave up and dipped the thick shakes out of the cup with the straws. It wasn't a problem, though, it only prolonged the pleasure.

Now it was time for the ultimate pleasure. We rode silently to town, parked in the municipal parking lot, and walked to the Carnival. The lights, sounds (calliope music and barkers), and smells bombarded us. The midway was still muddy from the week of rain, and there was sawdust in the muddiest spots. We could smell the hot dogs with onions cooking. They smelled so good, but when I watched as people bought the hot dogs, there was nothing on the bun but a wiener. The proprietors of the hot dog stand just fried onions to attract customers. We were glad that we had eaten at the Sterling, until we rode the Tilt-a-Whirl. John had to run between two tents and vomit. Dad didn't say anything; he just handed John the clean, but dingy, blue and white cotton handkerchief that he always carried.

     As we continued, we walked past the "games of chance". There was a man urging Dad to shoot at ducks, but Dad just acted like he was deaf. Two teenagers were throwing footballs through tires. They had won so many stuffed tigers that the "carnie" told them to leave.   I heard at school the next Monday that my friend Sherry's older brother had lost more than $200 rolling dice and moving markers toward a goal. The closer he got to the goal, the more money he had to bet. He thought he was going to win a TV, but he lost his whole paycheck.

     The most tantalizing part of the Carnival was the sideshows—the hermaphrodite, the snake-eating woman, the fire eater, and, of course, the "hoochie koochie" show. We stood outside of each tent as the barker told of the amazing things we could see inside. The "hoochie koochie" girls danced on stage, dressed in harem garb. As we stood on the fringe of the crowd, Stan Stillmore came out of the "hoochie koochie" show.

"Did they really take their clothes off?" Dad asked when he thought we couldn't hear.

"Lord, yes, and the pretty one took this here toboggan off my head and rubbed it between her legs. Of course, she had a G-string on, but I am never going to wash this here hat."

Stan continued, "And, my brother got up on the stage with the girls and danced 'til they threw him out. It was a great show!" He still had a dazed grin as he walked away.

Dad just shook his head and laughed, while John and I were dumbfounded. It had been quite a day.

May, 1960, was the time for the Primary Election. The Democrat John F. Kennedy was running against the Republican candidate, former Vice-President Richard Nixon. West Virginia was important to the Kennedy Campaign. West Virginia was a "yellow dog Democrat state", which meant that a yellow dog would be elected, if it ran on the "Democrat" ticket. But there was one obstacle to Kennedy's election in West Virginia. Kennedy was a Catholic, and many people, including Mom, did not want to vote for him because of his religion. They thought that because Catholics owed allegiance to the Pope, that the Pope would have some authority over our country.

So, in May, John F. Kennedy and his entourage came to Welch, West Virginia, to campaign. He stayed at the Carter Hotel, the only hotel in Welch. He made speeches and shook hands. He borrowed a dime for a phone call from Mom's friend Ruth, the desk clerk at the Carter Hotel, and never repaid it.

It was rumored that all of the brothels in Cinder Bottom, in Keystone (near Welch) were closed for the duration of Kennedy's visit. It was assumed that the brothels would give our area a bad image for visiting politicians, but it was later rumored that the brothels were closed to the public in order to give Kennedy's entourage complete access to the amenities. That rumor just added to Mom's determination to vote Republican for the first time.

As the lilacs bloomed, Mom would cut some from the bush in our yard so that I could take a bouquet to my teacher. We had taken our achievement tests, and it was time to determine who would pass to the next grade. On the last day of school, it was still a mystery if we had passed or not because the report cards were mailed to the parents three or four days later. Each morning I would walk around the curve, down the church steps, past the playground, along the broken sidewalk, being careful not to "step on a crack and break my mother's back" (which was really hard), and to the tin-sided post office on the banks of Tug River. Because we got our mail "General

Delivery", I politely stepped up to the wire covered window and said, "Any mail for Vandells?" The postmistress (either Lily Neil or Mrs. Blevins) would turn around and look behind her into a cubby marked with a V, sort through all of the envelopes, and pull out mail for the Vandells. When the report card finally arrived in the brown envelope, addressed with the perfect handwriting of Miss Propst, I gingerly carried it home for Mom to read.

With relief I listened to her say, "You passed," to John and to me. All that day, as we encountered our friends on Spruce Street, we would be greeted with the question, "Did you pass?" We would act like it was no big deal as we said, "Yes, did you?" Nobody on Spruce Street ever failed to pass to the next grade. That only happened to kids like Randy Cochran or Oscar's kids.

The last weekend in May, while the rest of the country celebrated Memorial Day, our family celebrated "Decoration Day", the day when we would visit the graves of deceased relatives and decorate them with wreaths and cut flowers. Aunt Tootsie and Uncle Ray came from Princeton. (Tootsie had been married to Archie Tramel, but he died in 1948 from injuries he received in a mining accident. Now she was married to Ray.) They were different from my parents because Uncle Ray smoked cigarettes that he made himself by pouring tobacco from a red Prince Albert can into small tissue papers. Then, he'd lick the edge of the paper to make it stick. He also had tattoos of a woman and an anchor on his arms. Tootsie had pierced ears and wore large gold hoop earrings that would swing when she began to shake her head as she spoke. I thought the earrings were beautiful because Mom wore no jewelry at all. Tootsie always greeted me by saying, "And here's Little Tru-Tru."

One time I asked Mom, whose name was Virginia Alice (but everyone called her "Sis"), why her older sister was given the unusual name of "Tootsie". She said that when Tootsie was born, her parents could not agree on a name. Her mother wanted the baby to be called Grace Mae, and her father wanted to name her Tootsie. So, they wrote the two choices on a stick and threw the stick into the air.

Whatever name was on the top when the stick landed would be the name given to the baby girl. The stick landed with the name "Grace Mae" on top; so, that was the legal name given to the baby. However, they called her Tootsie as she became a little girl, and when she became an adult, Tootsie had her name changed on her birth certificate to match what everyone called her.

On Memorial Day we all loaded up in cars, including the aunts and uncles, and drove through Welch and over Premier Mountain, about eleven miles, to the Roderfield Cemetery. At the entrance of the cemetery we passed unpainted houses with dirty bikes, rusty tricycles, and dirty children in the yards. I felt sorry for kids who had to live so close to a graveyard.

Once in the cemetery, we put artificial wreaths purchased at G. C. Murphy's Department Store on the graves of Papaw, Archie Tramel (Tootsie's first husband), "Old Man Jim Bromfield", and others who had died before I had been born. We were always careful not to step on any of the graves and to be respectful and quiet in the cemetery. Then, as always, we met Uncle Buddy and Aunt Anna Belle at the family grave plots, and things got louder and happier.

Uncle Buddy said, "When I am buried here, I want a bench for a tombstone, so you all can have a place to sit down when you all come here." We all laughed at that because nobody had a bench for a tombstone. They were all white marble or gray granite vertical stones, marking the head of each grave. Some had angels or lambs on them, but there were definitely no benches.

On Monday, May 31 (Decoration Day), Mom, John, and I walked about a mile to Uncle Buddy's and Aunt Anna Belle's house. Mom carried red Japanese quinces cut from the bush in the back yard. She had put them in a quart Mason jar of water. When we arrived at Buddy's and Anna Belle's house, we all set off up rutted the dirt road to the cemetery at the top of the mountain. Buddy carried a shovel, a small axe, and a hoe, and Anna Belle a jar of yellow flowers cut from her own yard.

As we walked, the kids ran ahead, looking for flowers and blackberries, which weren't ripe yet. We always "kept our eyes peeled" for snakes. We walked past the Hemphill slate dump, where many years before the mine cars dumped the slate and rock refuse from the mining process over the hill. The slate dump was a hill of gray rock with a few tenacious bushes clinging to the side of the hill.

At the bottom of the shady hill was a small stagnant pond with green slime covering the murky water. Beside the slate dump we made a hairpin turn onto a road that was not only rutted, but also overgrown. (Now we knew why Buddy had brought the axe.) Sharp briers clawed at our ankles and legs, and sweat bees and gnats buzzed around our sweaty faces, but we kept on climbing.

Finally, out of breath and sweaty, we reached the summit of the mountain. I expected to see a neatly manicured cemetery with upright tombstones like Roderfield. What we saw was an overgrown area with three or four small stone tombstones and three or four small boulders that supposedly marked graves. It was, however, a shaded, quiet, almost sacred place. The leaves of the tall oak and poplar trees formed a semi-solid roof that allowed speckles of light to be cast on the forest floor that was covered with soft brown rotting leaves and green weeds and bushes. The only sounds were birds chirping far off and our muted voices as we stared at the majestic greenness and soft brown tones of the woods, following the slope of the hill until we could see the three distinct "hollers" of Hemphill below us.

    The kids walked around and looked at the few marked graves (Oscar's baby boy who had died just a couple of years ago, and six-year-old Eddie Love who had drowned in Tug River last spring). These graves were marked with small boulders, not like the monuments I had seen at Roderfield. The names were scratched into the surface of the rough rock. The adults walked and looked to try to find the site of the graves of their mother and her newborn son, buried in November, 1928. Finally, they decided that the graves were two slightly sunken, overgrown areas on the "point" that overlooked all of Hemphill.

    Buddy began to cut the briers, weeds, and shrubs with the axe, while the rest of us dragged the brush to the edge of the hill and threw it over. With the undergrowth removed, Buddy used the shovel and hoe to mound dirt on the unmarked graves. They now looked like real graves. Finally, Anna Belle and Mom put the flowers in the Mason jars on each grave, and the kids added some flowers that we had picked along the way—Queen Anne's lace, and dandelions. Tired and satisfied, we left the chapel-like cemetery.

    Going downhill was somewhat easier; however, parts were so steep that we needed to grip with our toes to keep from tumbling down headfirst. As we walked at a leisurely pace, I asked Mom how her mother and baby brother had died so long ago. She said that she was only ten years old at the time and that she did not remember much about it. But then, like a mountain stream, the words began to flow, slow at first, then flowing, then cascading. This is the story she told.

When it was time for the baby to be born, the company doctor came to the house on the hill in Hemphill. He brought his black doctor's bag and a rubber sheet to protect the bed and sheets. He delivered the baby in the back bedroom and left. (Some of the neighbors would wash the rubber sheet and return it to the doctor's office the next week, as had been done by the previous user.) Within hours, my mother, Maggie, became very weak. She could not eat, and she could not nurse the baby. Her body became hot with fever, and she became weaker and weaker. Then, diarrhea developed. Of course, she could not walk up on the hill to the "Johnny-house"; she could not even get out of bed to use the white enameled "slop jar" beside the bed. The brown waste was projected quickly and violently from her fever-wracked body onto the floral wallpaper. Then it ran down the wall, like watery brown paint. An ambulance was called to take my mother and the baby, Anthony, to Grace Hospital in Welch. I secretly knew then, that I would never see my mother again.

My dad, Tom Bromfield, spent the next two days with his wife as she lay suffering in a ward filled with rows of metal hospital beds containing other sick women at Grace Hospital in Welch. On Saturday morning he walked home from the hospital *and told my sister Tootsie to find me. We needed to go to the hospital quickly. As usual, I was playing "house" with my best friend Ruby when Tootsie finally found me. We quickly changed out of our "play clothes" and walked the two miles through town and across the bridge to the large brown brick building. We walked up the outer stone steps, through the shiny tiled hallway, and up the stairs to the second floor ward. From the stairway landing we could see a nurse standing at the top of the steps. She slowly shook her head, and we knew we were too late. We would never see Mother again.*

That very day, Tom carried a small casket on his shoulder up onto the mountain top. It contained the body of his baby boy. There, some family and friends helped him bury Baby Anthony. Maggie was buried beside her baby three days later. There was no money for headstones. Their passing would be marked only in memories.

With the death of Maggie, it became twelve-year old Tootsie's responsibility to take care of the younger children and the house. She had to do everything from wash and change the diapers of her two-year-old brother to pack her Dad's dinner bucket and cook and clean for the family. So, at age twelve, Tootsie had to drop out of school. When the principal of the Welch School and the truant officer came to see why Tootsie was not attending school, her father said, "I have tried and tried to find a lady to come in and take care of the kids, but you know that no decent woman would do that because it just wouldn't 'look right' for a woman to keep house for a widower. So, if you can find someone to help me take care of these kids, that would be great. Otherwise, Tootsie has to stay home and do it." Tom and Tootsie never heard from the principal again, and Tootsie never went back to school. To this day, she says that she has never regretted quitting school.

CHAPTER 3

"Jolly, Boy! Hey, Jolly Boy; come over here, over here!" All of the kids on Spruce Street had hurried to the bank of Tug River to yell across into "colored camp", a row of white houses originally built for African-American coal workers. Now the houses were owned by those same workers, or other African American families. We had heard the tinkling music in the white paneled truck that signaled the true arrival of summer. The ice cream truck with "Jolly Boy" and a smiling face painted on it was making its way up the road on the other side of the river, stopping often to distribute treats like ice cream sandwiches, orange push-ups, and Popsicles and to take dimes in payment.

This June was hot, maybe even hot enough for the city of Bluefield, located about forty miles away, to give away free lemonade on each street corner. Bluefield advertised itself as "Nature's Air Conditioned City"; so if the temperature ever got above ninety degrees, the city gave away free lemonade. It was a big deal, if it got "lemonade hot."

As we watched "Jolly Boy" drive out of view on the other side of the river, we hoped that he would go up to the county road and turn around to come to Spruce Street, but "Jolly Boy" rarely came. Maybe it was because Spruce Street was a narrow, dead end street that was hard to navigate. Or, maybe it was because there weren't many children on

Spruce Street and there were even fewer dimes that summer.

June was the month we attended Vacation Bible School. Mom, John, and I walked from our house on Spruce Street to the new brick church building on Stewart Street beside the Foremost Milk Plant. We walked more than a mile to and from the First Church of God, but there was no question about attending every day because Mom was the director of the one-week session of Bible School.

We always started with all of the children meeting in the sanctuary listening to the rules, the "theme" for the week and learning the official song of that year's Bible School. Then, we went to our small classrooms for a Bible story lesson. It was hard fitting ten or twelve children around a small table, but they did it, and we learned about parables, being "fishers of men", and "loving one another". (I just hoped that didn't mean Randy Cochran and Cousin Oscar's raggedy kids too.)

Susan cried every morning, but she would calm down by the time we went to the bathroom and had an outside play time. We played circle games (drop the handkerchief or duck, duck, goose) on the small front lawn of the church or in the "red dog" (charred slate) covered parking lot, located past one house up the street from the church. Next, we always had red Kool-aid and store-bought cookies, the hard, cheap kind, placed on napkins. After that, we went to the fellowship hall to sing the songs that Mrs.Tucker, the music director, had planned for us to sing at the closing program on the last day of Bible School. This year we sang "None is Like God" every day, since it was the theme song of this year's Bible School, as well as "Do Lord" and "Jesus Loves the Little Children".

Then came the highlight of Bible School—the craft. We usually made something with Popsicle sticks—a small box or a picture frame. We even planted grass seeds on a cotton ball in an eggshell to show that God uses small things to make miracles. By the end of the week, grass was growing in that eggshell!

At noon, the bell rang, and we gathered our crafts and Mom's books and headed back to Hemphill, walking past the Welch Emergency Hospital, Yeager Ford Sales, the Board of Education Building, across the bridge that went over the railroad tracks. We could peer into the dark tunnel that was beside the bridge and remember stories of boys who dared take a shortcut through the tunnel. They would have to step into shallow "man holes" cut into the tunnel walls and let the speeding train pass within inches of their faces, sucking the very breath from their lungs. I laughed to myself as I thought about the only time I had actually seen two scrawny shirtless boys coming out of the tunnel. A man was chasing them through the tunnel with a shot gun. It seems that they had discovered his stash of old brown bleach bottles filled with moonshine on the hill above the tunnel, and he was defending his property. He was yelling and shooting, but, thankfully, he could not catch up with the adventurous boys.

    We walked around the county road past Angelo's and Tony's "jottem down store" onto Spruce Street for an afternoon of play. Before we could change into play clothes and eat lunch, Larry knocked on the back door and said, "Is John Bandell home? Can he come out?" Before we could answer, John would have his Matchbox cars in his hands, and they would be off to build roads in Larry's back yard.

    After a tuna fish sandwich and grape Kool-aid, I got my "jack rocks" and ball and went to find my best friend Debbie. We played on her front porch for hours. I threw the jacks up, put the backs of my hands together and caught some, and then threw them up again and caught some more in my cupped hands. The three that landed on the porch were picked up by "onesies" while I threw the small red rubber ball up. I continued the same ritual and picked up by "twosies and "threesies", until I failed to pick up all of the metal jacks on the "foursies". Then, it was Debbie's turn. Since there were ten jacks we played to "tensies", and then we got fancy, putting "cows in the barn" and "going around the world". We played until our little fingers and the sides of our hands were black with the dirt that was imbedded in the cement porch. We liked playing on Debbie's porch because she had the only cement porch on Spruce Street. Our wooden porch caused the ball to bounce unpredictably, and splinters were a common hazard when playing jacks.

After supper, Debbie, her sister Cathy, and I jumped rope, stringing the long rope across the street. Cathy and I turned as Debbie ran into the rope. We then chanted:
Cinderella, dressed in yella'
Went upstairs to kiss her fella'
Made a mistake, kissed a snake,
How many doctors did it take?
1, 2, 3, 4, 5, 6, 7, 8, 9, 10—HOT
Cathy and I turned the rope faster and faster until Debbie missed and it was my turn to jump.

When we were really hot and sweaty, we enlisted John, Larry, and Jerry and played "rotten egg" on the rock wall at the back of our yard. As usual, Jerry got mad and started a "rock fight", throwing rocks at anyone in sight until I got hit, cried and went home to the protection of Mom. Rock fights were not allowed; so it was time to take a bath and get ready for bed. Besides, by this time, the street lights had come on, and everyone knew that that was the signal that playtime was over for the day.

One of John's favorite activities was throwing rocks in Tug River to see if he could get them to the other side, where the "colored camp" was located. While some people used the term n----- camp for the area where the African American residents of Hemphill lived, Mom insisted that we use the term "colored" (a polite term at that time) when speaking about our neighbors across the river. John had to be stealthy about his rock throwing because Mom did not allow it. She envisioned John hurling a rock so hard that the force would project him right into the black, contaminated water. The river was the receiver of sewage, which flowed directly from all houses located on its banks from Welch through all of Hemphill, including ours. On washday, we watched the gray water gush from the pipe on the riverbank as the washing machine emptied and refilled. The water was black from the coal refuse from mines located on branches of the Tug, many miles upstream at Gary and Keystone. The river was hardly ever more that two feet deep; so most of the time the river contained as much waste product as actual water.

"Hairplane, hairplane," Larry shouted. The sound of an airplane flying over Hemphill was time to stop any activity, shade our eyes and try to see the silver glint in the summer sky. Sometimes we were stopped in our tracks by a sonic boom that sounded like thunder. When I asked Mom what made that thunderous sound on such a sunny day, she replied, "A plane is flying faster that the speed of sound. Amazing, isn't it?"

During June and July our play might be interrupted by the sound of a lone helicopter spraying the power lines. The glass and silver "whirlybird" spewed its strong acrid smelling mist along the power lines to kill the vegetation around and under the wires. By the next day, the smell was still faintly there, and the weeds and small trees had already begun to dry up and turn brown.

Bike riding was a favorite pastime for kids on Spruce Street. They rode carefully up and down the street, being careful not to get near cars parked on the narrow strips of dirt dumped beside the river to provide enough space for a car. If a car came down the one-lane street, someone would yell, "Car", and the bike riders would stop and try to find a wide spot to get out of the narrow street.

I did not own a bike; therefore, I did not learn to ride one until my friend Debbie let me ride a green eighteen-inch bike that she had outgrown. Dad had made a contraption for me to ride called a "jumping jack". I sat on the seat (a board screwed to the frame) and pushed down on a bar with my feet. As I pushed down, the seat rose and the rust and burgundy colored contraption moved forward. My jumping jack had three wheels and moved incredibly slowly; so it was just not the same as the blue two-wheeler that Debbie had.

When dusk arrived, we knew it was time to go home. As I stepped directly from the street onto the cement steps, past the landing and up steps onto the front porch, I saw Dad sitting there in the dark with a "gnat smoke" perched on the wide banister. Dad had put old socks into a one pound coffee can and lit them with a match. The smoldering wool made a pungent smoke that drove away gnats and mosquitoes, and some people, too.

"Why don't you catch some of them lightning bugs? They're all over the yard there," Dad said.

I ran into the house and asked Mom if I could have a jar. John followed me as I set the jar on the front steps and ran into the grassy side yard. It was hilly, so we had to watch our step as we cupped the fireflies in our hands and carefully carried them, one by one, back to the jar. They lit up the jar like a lantern. Some of the older girls on Spruce Street pulled the yellow tails off the bugs and put them on their ears like luminous earrings, but I always released them from the jar before going inside for the night. If I forgot and left them in the jar overnight (the jar had holes in the lid to allow the bugs to breathe), the glowing fireflies looked just like any other annoying insect in the daylight.

When June boredom set in the kids looked for other pastimes. Playing ball was usually out of the question because after very few throws or hits, the ball would land in Tug River and become the lucky find of another kid downstream. So, we played in the old "firehouse", a small white building with green trim that the coal company had used to store fire hoses during the "coal boom". Parents tried to keep kids from playing in the empty wooden garage-like building, because it stood on stilts on the river bank and hung precariously over the river. But, each summer, the kids would knock a hole in the side of the building and crawl inside. It was a perfect clubhouse. After a few days, the adults would give up, and open the big doors for a time. Then, mysteriously, the hole would be patched up and the doors locked again.

      Then came the big adventure of the summer. Our older neighbor Jerry and his older brother built a wagon of boards and leftover wheels from broken wagons, doll carriages, or tricycles. The long wooden contraption had a wide flat board for a seat, and it was steered by a rope connected to the front "axle" that swiveled on a large nail. There were no brakes. Each kid took a turn riding down the steep hill in Jerry's yard. Finally, it was my turn. I sat down on the hard seat with each foot stationed on the front wooden axle. I took the reins, and Jerry gave a big push. The wagon rattled and bumped as it raced down the hill. My teeth rattled, my hair was blowing back, and my brain became scrambled. At the bottom of the hill, I was supposed to put my feet down and drag them until the wagon stopped. I was so terrified with the ride that the wagon jumped right into the street, crossed it and landed on the riverbank. All of the kids came and pulled me out of the bushes, but Jerry would not let me ride his wagon again, for which I was very grateful.

      On any given summer afternoon Mom summoned me to come inside, get the "store bill" (list) and go to Quattrone's Grocery Store, a bigger, more well-stocked store than Stafford's Grocery. The list, written in pencil on the back of an old envelope contained only a few items—a long loaf of bread, a half-gallon of milk (in a wax covered cardboard carton), and a half pound of bologna, sliced thin so Mom could make more sandwiches with it. I always smiled when I read the word "bologna", remembering that Uncle Buddy called it "coal miners' steak." At the bottom of the list was written "a nickel's worth of penny candy."

      Clutching the list, I walked up Spruce Street, around the curve, down the familiar church steps, past the Methodist Church, and by the playground. Since it was summer, the playground, surrounded by a high cyclone fence, was open, and the sounds bombarded my ears.

      There was the thud of a bouncing basketball and the grunts of sweaty bigger boys as they thrust the ball toward the rusty hoop with no net. (This was one of the few activities in Hemphill where both black and white boys played, talked, and laughed together.) There was the laughter of kids being pushed on the large wooden board swings with thick blackened chains or running and jumping on the round wooden merry-go-round with worn metal rails that left a distinctive metallic smell on sweaty hands. But, the most distinctive sound of the Hemphill Playground was the rings. Large metal rings were fastened to the top of a tall pole with heavy metal chains. The rings were designed to turn around as children grabbed onto them and ran around the pole. Then, the kids took their feet off the ground and swung out horizontally into the air. As kids let go of the heavy rings, they clanged loudly. Or, on a windy day, the clang of the empty rings could be heard all over Hemphill.

    I continued up the uneven sidewalk, past the Blue Swan (a "colored beer joint"). It was rumored that "bad girls" lived upstairs, but I did not know what kind of bad things they could have done. I passed the post office, up the wide, but uneven concrete step onto the porch of Quattrone's Grocery, called Patsy's by older folks because the original owner was Patsy (Pasquale) Quattrone. I noticed that the kerosene pump on the front porch was locked. I guess there is no need for "coal oil" to heat houses during the summer. On the right was the swinging bridge that crossed Tug River, and on the left across the narrow street was a three story dark red brick apartment building with a wooden porch. That was the building where the widow Claudia Carmona sold "bootleg" whiskey during Prohibition Days in the 1930's. From the porch, she let down a basket on a rope. When a customer put money in the basket, she pulled it up, and lowered it back down with "white lightning" in it. That is how she supported her seven children during the Depression.

    I reached for the blackened metal of the green framed screen door of the store. I looked up into the very back of the store, where a small balcony contained the office that Dante and his spinster sister Eleanor Quattrone used for store business—inventory, billing, and such. Upon entering the dark space, I was immediately greeted by the odor of fruits and vegetables that were in the early stages of decay. Lettuce, cabbage, squash, tomatoes, and green beans were piled high on the white cooler shelves. Directly across from the cooler was the metal green painted counter, but there was no paint on the top of the counter. It had been rubbed down to the bare gray tin by thousands, even millions, of transactions. By the cash register there, bespectacled Eleanor stood with her long clean white apron over her faded striped button-up dress. I timidly handed her the crumpled list. She often spoke harshly to kids in the store; so I was very careful not to cause any problem for her.

    Eleanor took the list and immediately went to the meat case to cut the bologna from a large cylindrical tube wrapped in red waxy paper. I didn't follow her because the white glassed meat case in the back of the store smelled like slightly rotten bloody meat and very strong fish. As she headed past the bread and "lunch cakes" (Hostess brand Twinkies, Sno-balls, cupcakes, and oatmeal cakes), she called back to me, "Go on over behind the candy counter and get a nickel's worth of penny candy."

    I eagerly walked on the blackened bare wood floors to the right, past the open freezer that contained Popsicles, Fudgesicles, Dreamsicles, Drumsticks, and ice cream sandwiches. I knew I could not even look at those because Popsicles and Dreamsicles cost six cents. In the darkened back was the "pop case", an open electric cooler containing glass bottles of RC's, Root Beers, Pepsis, and any other variety of sweet drink. Beside the "pop case" was the ice cream freezer, where Eleanor or her helper Mary would take a metal scoop from a plastic bucket of water, dip out a scoop of vanilla, chocolate, strawberry, or maple nut ice cream and put it onto a sugar or wafer cone for the price of five cents.

    But I was not interested in ice cream on this day. The candy counter was a wood and glass case with three shelves. The candy was visible from the aisles in the store, but I was allowed to go behind the glass case, slide the glass door open and choose the "penny candy" that was displayed in boxes. I could not decide. I could get a Hershey bar, or an Almond Joy, but Mom had written penny candy; so that is what I would get. I looked at each treasure—Kits (four pieces of taffy for a penny), square Double Bubble Bubblegum with tiny folded comics, three sticks of bubble gum in a blue wrapper for a penny, three wax bottles of syrupy liquid called "soda pop", and on and on. I finally decided on a red Safety pop, two fireballs, a Mary Jane, and the three sticks of gum. I put the candy in one of the small brown bags that lay on top of the glass counter and took my treasure to the cash register.

    Eleanor took my bag of candy and counted the pieces. Then she   pulled a brown paper bag from beneath the counter, wrote the cost of each item on Mom's list on the outside of the bag, added tax, and wrote the total. Then she said, "Tell your Mama that I put it on the book." That meant that she wrote the total in a composition book, and that she would bill Mom and Dad at the end of the month. I carried the bag from the store, with my "poke" of penny candy in my free hand. Quickly, I walked down the big steps, careful to keep my balance. I walked past Quattrone's storage building, which was a beer joint called Pop's Cozy Corner during Hemphill's war-time heyday, and into the post office. Of course, I said to Lily Neil, "Any mail for Vandells?" She turned and searched through the envelopes in the "V" cubby and shook her head.

  Now, I could enjoy the wages for my trip to the store. As I walked up the broken sidewalk, with the cherry safety pop (a lollipop with a looped string instead of a stick) in my mouth, I heard my older brother Ron talking to Macon Bush. I heard Macon say as he grinned, showing white teeth between his full black lips, "Hey Ronnie, loan me a 'nilkel' so I can buy a 'belverage'." I knew Ron didn't have a nickel. After all, it was 1960 in Hemphill.

Inside the Spruce Street house

CHAPTER 4

Just like in the rest of America, the Fourth of July meant picnics and fireworks in Hemphill. I walked out onto the small front porch, and Dad was sitting in the heavy steel cushioned chair that bounced, rather than rocked. He had bought it in 1943, and it had layers and layers of various colors of paint on it, but it was currently painted bright green. He was watching an old truck with wooden sides as it slowly drove up the road in "colored camp" across the river. The truck stopped, and several people, kids and adults, came out to the truck carrying boxes and baskets. One man was carrying a watermelon.

"They are going on a picnic," Dad said, "probably to Pinnacle Rock, up near Bluefield."

"Are we going anywhere today?" I cautiously asked.

"We might go on a weenie roast to Poplar Grove Park."

Just then, I saw my older brother Ron walking toward us carrying a brown bag.

"Ronnie's been to Quattrone's to get the ice cream. You know, they only open for two hours on the Fourth of July so that people who don't have freezers can buy ice cream for the Fourth. They have been doing that since Patsy Quattrone opened the store back before the Depression."

"Was Patsy Dante's and Eleanor's father?"

"Yeah, he had several children—raised 'em in the apartment right above the store."

"Have you ever seen the inside of the apartment?" I attentively asked.

"Only once. When Ol' Man Patsy died, I went to the wake up over the store. The dark stairs up to the apartment were narrow and steep, and there was a sharp turn in them. When Douglas Mortuary brought Ol' Man Patsy's body in the casket to the apartment for the wake, they couldn't get the casket around the sharp turn. So, they took Patsy out of the casket, and carried him up to the apartment. When I went to the wake, he was layin' there on a couch, just like he was asleep."

I ran inside to check out the ice cream—butter pecan—one of the best flavors sold. Mom took a big spoon and dipped the ice cream into bowls for each of us. I took mine, and a bigger serving for Dad, onto the front porch.

"Every Fourth of July when we have ice cream, I think of that weenie roast we had at Poplar Grove Park," Dad said with a sly grin.

"When was that?" I asked, wondering why he was grinning.

"Well, you must have been a little baby, because Archie (my cousin who was two years older than I was) was just a little boy. Your Uncles Buddy and Donnie and their families and all of us went on a weenie roast. Buddy and Donnie had bought a big five-gallon tub of butter pecan ice cream. You know, the kind in the round cardboard carton. When they opened it up to serve it, it was a little too hard to dip. So, they 'let it set' awhile. The next thing we knew, little Archie was 'peeing' in that ice cream."

"We all screamed and yelled at him to stop, but Buddy said, 'Aw, we can't waste this whole carton of ice cream, since the Fourth of July is the only time we get to eat it,' and he turned the container upside down and scooped the precious treat out of the bottom."

"Every time I eat butter pecan ice cream I think of that time," Dad said. "You know, you can't waste something as expensive and rare as ice cream."

In late afternoon, I saw the truck returning, full of "colored folks", laughing and singing. You could hear them from our porch. "They must have had a great time." I thought.

We had a good time too, with our ice cream and, of course, watermelon on the Fourth of July. It didn't take much to make us happy in Hemphill in 1960.

    Summertime was hot, but there was always a cool shady place to sit and think, like under the lilac bush that hung over and formed a cool shady cave. It was great for hiding from Mom when she called me to come to supper. However, if I hid for too long, the nearby forsythia bush made great little thin switches for "whoopin'" my bare legs, not to mention a hairbrush or flyswatter. Mom would quickly punish infractions of family law, especially "sassing", which was my most common offense.

    Summer rain showers provided great fun. Dad would say, "I see a storm comin' over the mountain; better make a tent. That is what you are supposed to do when it rains."

    We never knew why we were supposed to make a tent, but John and I quickly looked for old quilts and blankets. Then we turned the porch rocker and other chairs over, and covered them with the blankets. We spent hours crawling in and out of the dark, musty-smelling "tents", having snacks, playing checkers, and just giggling and talking. But, when thunder and lightning came, it was time to take down the "tents" and go inside. That was the boring time because everybody knew that you could not use the telephone, watch television, or take a bath during a thunderstorm.

Sunday mornings broke the monotony of summer. While weekday breakfasts usually consisted of oatmeal, cream of wheat, Cheerios, Jets cereal, soft boiled eggs and toast, or "deviled ham" (called "boogerman ham" by Dad), Sunday breakfast was different. I always woke up earlier than everyone else. Because there was nothing on TV, except the test pattern and a whining sound, I "pilfered" through drawers to find interesting things, and I always looked for the leftover Saturday night candy from Murphy's Department Store.

Each Saturday afternoon or evening, Dad went to the glass candy counter at Murphy's and chose three or four kinds of candy and some warm roasted Spanish peanuts. Murphy's had no air conditioning; so, the summer candy differed from the candy sold during cooler weather. In the winter, there might be chunks of Hershey's chocolate, small Clark bars, chocolate covered peanuts or peanut clusters. But, in the summer, there were jellied orange slices, maple "peach pits", and bridge mix. Always, Dad brought home three small white bags, each containing a quarter or half pound of candy, and a red and white striped bag of nuts, with the grease already bleeding through the bag. Dad called it "television candy", and we all shared as we watched "Porter Wagoner", "Lawrence Welk", and "Perry Mason" on the rounded screen of the black and white console TV.

By Sunday morning, only a few pieces of each candy and very few peanuts were left in each small bag—always Bridge mix and orange slices. I was alone in the big, quiet house with the goodies, and I ate to my stomach's content. By the time Mom got up to start breakfast, I was back upstairs to start getting ready for church.

    Sunday morning breakfast began with the smell of frying bacon and coffee perking in the slim silver electric percolator. Then Mom mixed up flour, Crisco, baking powder, and buttermilk, rolled the mixture out on a "biscuit board", kneaded it, rolled it out, and cut round shapes with a small Carnation cream can. (The empty can had been heated, and then the top was knocked off, forming a sharp, circular cutting edge.) With her fingers, she then slathered a baking sheet with streaks of Crisco, put the doughy biscuits on it, and put them in the oven. Then she quickly fried an egg for each of us, and made sawmill gravy. It was all orchestrated so that each part of the magnificent breakfast was done at the same time. As she put the biscuits in a napkin-lined basket, the eggs on a plate, she was calling the family to breakfast. I had already set the table and put the butter, home-made blackberry preserves, honey, and salt and pepper on the table.

    Meals in the house on Spruce Street were enjoyed in the breakfast nook, nestled between the kitchen and the dining room. The built-in table and tall-backed white benches provided cozy seating for all of us, except John, who sat on a tall gray vinyl and chrome stool at the end of the table. After we all sat down, I said grace, "God is great; God is good. Let us thank him for our food. Amen."

Then Dad said, "Pass the 'catheads' (what he called biscuits), and 'paste'" (gravy). Even though he said this every Sunday, we always laughed.

Of course I ate an egg, but the best part of the breakfast was breaking the biscuits into small pieces, covering them with gravy, and crumbling bacon on the top. Dad called this a "masterpiece", and I enjoyed every morsel, even as the gravy began to cool and thicken on my plate.

After clearing the table, we got ready for Sunday School and the church service that followed.   My older sister Janice would wash the dishes after church. She would run water in the shallow porcelain coated cast iron sink, pour Cheer detergent in the water, wash each dish, and put it in the red wire drainer. It was my job to dry the dishes as she washed. I always had an excuse to delay the job (use the bathroom, wash my hands, find a clean dish towel, whatever), but I never completely got out of doing the chore.

Dressed in our best clothes, Dad drove us to the First Church of God on Stewart Street every Sunday and Wednesday. Mom wore her one nice navy blue shirt waist dress with high heeled shoes. Every other day, she wore a "house dress", faded to a non-descript color with socks or house shoes. But, not on Sunday.

At the top of the hill, where Spruce Street met the county road, we stopped and picked up Lily Neil, who lived around the county road on Whaley Hill, and Sister Willis, who lived in an unpainted shack right at the top of Spruce Street. Lily, the Hemphill postmistress, was a short lady with thin, white hair, pulled back in a bun. She always wore a purple dress and a purple hat, and she was famous for her entertainment at church dinners. She played "This Ole House" on a pie pan and "Aloha Oe" by pinching her nose while humming. Sister Willis was the only "colored" person who attended the First Church of God. She always wore either a white or a black dress and matching hat. Lily and Sister Willis piled in the back seat with John and me, and we headed for church.

Dad stopped in the church parking lot, and we trooped out—all except Dad. We quietly walked up the sidewalk and into the entrance. This new brick structure was much nicer than the old white wooden building on the hill, which flooded in the basement and had several snakes that visited the Sunday School classrooms at times.

As Trudy Tucker played the organ and the choir, with my sister Janice in the front row, filed in, Mom, John, and I sat on the third row, behind Lily. We sang "Holy, Holy, Holy", and as we sang about "cherubim and seraphim" I wondered what they looked like. The offering was taken by Brother Wilson, Brother Snead, and Dude Tucker, who always said the same prayer after the offering. Mom quietly placed the white tithe envelope, which contained ten percent of Dad's meager pay, in the wooden offering plate, and then we sang "Praise God from Whom All Blessings Flow".

All of that was bearable for a kid, but the sermon was long and boring, and it was hot, even with the bottom panes of the stained glass windows pulled open. I stared at the large window above the glassed-in baptistery. It was a picture of Jesus in the Garden of Gethsemane, and "Not my will, but Thine be done," was printed beneath the picture. I began to fidget on the hard wooden church pew, but Mom calmed my squirming with a pinch on the thigh. Then, she handed me a half stick of Wrigley's Spearmint gum. (She said that I made too much noise with a whole stick. Besides, the other half was given to John.) I continued to look at each stained glass window, because each one had been purchased by church members and, therefore, had different pictures and names on them. I reached into the rack on the back of Lily's pew and found the large cardboard fan on a stick. It had a picture of a girl in church (with gloves and a hat on—just like me), and on the back it had the name of funeral home that provided the fans each summer for the church—Fanning Funeral Home. Also, there was a smaller bell-shaped cardboard fan. I picked it up and pulled out the thumb tabs on the sides. It spread out into a large fan with a picture of a church in the woods on it. It was donated by

Douglas Mortuary. I fanned with the fans until Mom handed me a pen, and I drew and wrote on the bulletin until Brother Burger, the preacher, asked us to stand for prayer. I thought the service was almost over, but not so. We sang all four verses of "Coming Home" while the preacher talked about coming out of sin and sorrow and coming home to Jesus, but no one came to the altar in front of the church. So then, we sang all four verses of "Just As I Am". Still, no one came to the front of the church to repent of their sins. Finally, Brother Burger gave up, and asked Mom to say the benediction. She prayed softly and eloquently about God's love and protection, but best of all for me, it was a short prayer and church was over.

After shaking the young bespectacled preacher's hand, we headed to the car. Dad was there, right where we left him, and he didn't say a word about church lasting much longer than the allotted hour. He drove us to Hemphill, stopping at the top of Spruce Street to let the ladies get out of the car. "Thank ya, Mr. Van," Sister Willis said as she slowly got out of the car.

With Lily and Sister Willis gone, I asked, "Dad, why don't you ever go to church with us?"

He answered with a grin, "I do go to church with you. I go twice as much as you do. I go there to take you, and I go to pick you up."

CHAPTER 5

The crescendo and decrescendo of jar flies came in late summer. By then, the late night games of hide and seek and "hot tail" had led to bare legs covered with gnat and mosquito bites. Constant scratching of the nagging itches caused scabby sores. The remedy was Gentian Violet, poured from a brown bottle, swabbed on the sores, creating a brilliant purple design on tanned legs and arms. Mom warned, "Don't scratch those bites; you'll get 'fall sores'". But, we scratched anyway, and shamefully wore the purple splotches like tattoos gone awry.

One hot Saturday afternoon Mom, Dad, John, and I got into the pink and black Dodge to go visit Uncle Buddy, Aunt Anna Belle, and the cousins. We had to turn around on the end of Spruce Street, drive up the narrow street along the river, around the blind curve, and up the hill to the county road. Dad topped the hill carefully so that he could watch for cars coming around a big curve on the county road. He drove past Angelo's Barber Shop around the road. Although we could see Buddy and Anna Belle's hillside house from the county road, Dad had to drive up to the school bus stop (a space dug out of the side of the hill), back in, and turn the car around. Then, he drove down "Patsy's Hill", past Patsy Quattrone's store at the bottom and past the post office. He then drove past the playground, Stafford's Grocery, the big iron bridge over Tug River, made a sharp left turn and drove along beside the shallow river. Turning to cross the railroad tracks we rode past Mrs. May's school bus that had been converted into a house, complete with gingham curtains and a stove pipe sticking out of one window, continuing up the hill to Buddy's house. We drove up the narrow, rocky, unpaved road, and right up into the washed-out, rutted, sandy front yard.

     Buddy and Anna Belle lived in a gray four-room "company house" with an outdoor toilet perched on the hill behind the house. The house had unpainted boards nailed vertically underneath it as "underpinning", and the steps up to the house and to the toilet were just large smooth stones periodically imbedded into the hillside. It was not like our big sparkling white "boss's house" on Spruce Street, with its grassy side and back yards and green tiled bathroom. I secretly felt sorry for my cousins who lived in the small house with the smelly outhouse.

     As we drove up to the house, we saw Anna Belle carrying a "slop jar" up the path to the outhouse. She wore a pair of child's panties on her head to protect her hair during her chores. She greeted us with a big smile and friendly wave, as always. She quickly emptied the "slop jar", and came to greet us. (The panties had discreetly disappeared.) As Dad slipped off to find Buddy tinkering under the hood of his black 1948 Chevy "work car", we entered the clean kitchen with gray speckled linoleum with large red and black blocks. We sat at the gray formica-topped table in black wrought iron chairs.

Mom said, "I like those checkered curtains. Are they new?"

"Lord, no," said Anna Belle. "But I washed them last week, and hung them out on the line in the back yard. When I went to get them, they were gone. I looked all over, but I couldn't find them. Then, a couple of days later, I went up the hill to see Heddy about a recipe, and she had curtains in her kitchen, just like these here. I told her I had some just like those, and asked her where she got hers. She said that she bought them from Mrs. Bostic up the hill.

Well, I went up to see Mrs. Bostic, and when I asked her if she took my curtains, she started yelling and shoving. Lord, we started hitting and rolling on the porch. When I held her down on the porch, she 'fessed up to takin' my curtains and sellin' 'em to Heddy.

Well, I went home, and a few minutes later, Heddy brought my curtains back, and there they hang."

Mom laughed and said, "It's a good thing you and Buddy bought this house from the coal company. Remember how the company used to send women who couldn't get along in the coal camp down to Marytown to live? They sent ol' Mrs. Ryan and her family to Marytown, didn't they? And her husband had to walk all the way to Hemphill to work in the mines."

I listened in amazement. I thought it was pretty funny that someone would steal curtains, but I was secretly glad that we did not have thieves living on Spruce Street.

As the conversation moved on to more mundane subjects, Anna Belle asked Mom, "Sis, do you have any rhubarb?"

Mom answered, "No, Lacy (Dad's middle name) hasn't ever planted any."

Anna Belle continued, "Well, take this here mess of rhubarb I cut this morning, and make Lacy a good ol' rhubarb pie."

Mom gladly accepted the reddish, celery-looking stalks and said, "I might try making a rhubarb-strawberry pie, since Lacy brought some wild strawberries home in his lunch bucket yesterday."

I left the women in the kitchen as they wrapped the rhubarb in newspapers and went to find my cousin Connie. Cousin Connie, whom Dad called "Yella Hair" because of her long cornsilk colored hair, was my age and in the same grade as I was in school. Cousin Willard, whom Dad called "Black Will" because he had dark hair and a dark complexion like his mother's family, was just a year older than John.

Buddy and Anna Belle had five children, and now they had a new baby in a crib in the kids' room. I don't know how they fit all eight people in that small four-room house, clinging to the side of the hill like the thirty or forty other houses in the Warwick section of

Hemphill, but the house was always clean and filled with laughter and true warmth.

When it was time to leave, we backed out of the sloped dirt yard, drove up to a wide spot where the road forked, turned around and headed back through Hemphill. When we passed Newbery Chester's house, Dad said, "It must be safe to buy "shine" today. The sheets are hung on the clothesline with spaces between them. If the sheets are hung side-by-side with no spaces, it means that you should not come to the house to buy moonshine."

I had seen the Chesters buying twenty-five pound bags of sugar at Quattrone's, but I thought Mrs. Chester just made a lot of jam or pickles or something. Now I knew they were using that sugar to make illegal liquor.

Just then, we saw two grown women rolling in Mrs. Smith's flower garden in her front yard. They were yelling, scratching, and pulling hair. Dad stopped the car, but before he got through the gate, Mr. Smith had pulled them apart and told them to go home. Mrs. May picked up the gingham bonnet that she always wore and headed back to her school bus home, with curtains, a bed, a coal burning stove, chairs, and all of the comforts of home. Posie headed back up the hill to her house at the end of the road, and we never found out who, or what, had started the fight. I was just glad that nobody on Spruce Street made moonshine or fought in the yards.

September, 1960, when the beggar's lice (Velcro-like green burs) clung to socks and pants, was a time of pride for our family. My older brother Ron quit his job at Welch's Municipal Parking Lot and left for College. I am sure that Mom always thought of "college" with a capital "C" because even though my oldest brother Tom went to a two-year college on the GI Bill, before Ron, no one in our family had been to a four-year college. Ron was majoring in engineering at West Virginia Tech. I didn't know what engineering was, but it sounded important and intelligent.

When we heard the raspy sound of katydids each evening, Dad said it would be six weeks until the first frost, but John and I knew that the sound meant that it was time to go back to school at Welch Elementary School on Stewart Street. I started school in first grade at the old Welch School (grades one through twelve) on the hill overlooking downtown Welch, but two years earlier on a February night in 1957, the elementary building of that school burned. I was very upset, not about missing school for a few weeks, but because I wanted to be first to deliver Valentine cards to my classmates. So, I had already carefully placed Valentine cards, each containing a stick of Dentyne chewing gum, in the Valentine bags that we had hung on the wooden tray at the blackboard. When I heard about the school fire, I envisioned the flames lapping at the bags and the melted gum dripping in pink strings along the wall. A few weeks after the fire, we were sent to the almost completed new Welch Elementary School on Stewart Street, where we continued our education.

Other than shopping for Easter outfits, our only other time for new clothes was the beginning of school. Again, we walked to Welch and tried on dresses (or pants for boys) and new shoes and socks. Each fall Mom told the story of the time she got new shoes when she was in school. She always began the story the same way.

It was the fall after the spring I had diphtheria, lost all my hair, and almost died. My mother was dead, and my sister Tootsie was doing her best to raise us kids while my dad worked from sunup 'til sundown in the mines. When it was time for me to go the school, I had no shoes to wear. I had gone barefoot all summer, since last year's shoes were worn clean through. My dad put cardboard in the bottoms of the shoes to make them last until school was out.

Well, one Saturday right before school started, my dad came home from the company store with a pair of black lace-up brogans, two sizes too large for me.

"Well, I'll be," he declared. "I picked up the wrong size!"

The next Saturday, he took the shoes back to the company store. As he approached the counter, the clerk said, "H'lo Tom." She knew all of the miners and their families, since everybody shopped at the company store.

Tom answered, "H'lo. I got these here shoes last Saturday, and they are too big for my little girl to wear to school."

The clerk looked at him kindly. She knew that she had not sold a pair of large black lace-up shoes to Tom for his little girl. She knew that he had slipped them under his jacket before leaving the store the previous Saturday. She also knew how little miners made (about two dollars a day) during the "Hoover Times", and she knew that Tom had four little children to clothe and feed without the help of a wife. Her heart went out to him.

"Sure," she said. "Let's see if we have a nicer pair in Sis' size."

She rummaged through several pairs of shoes before coming up with a substantial pair in the right size. She handed them to my dad, and he left the store with new shoes for me to start school.

In 1960 my teacher was Mrs. Santoro. Each year the students were ability grouped, and the teachers took turns having different groups. Mrs. Santoro had the "high group" that year, thirty-five of us. Mrs. Colobro had the "middle group", where my cousin Connie was placed. All of the students knew which teacher had the high, middle and low groups, and I secretly felt proud of being in with the children of doctors and lawyers from Welch. However, the pride was short-lived when on the first day of school the teacher called each student's name and asked for a mailing address. I was always so ashamed to say,

"General Delivery, Hemphill". I would always follow with the words, "But I live in the Welch City limits," (which was true). It just didn't sound the same as a street address, like the other kids had.

  Last year in third grade, we had science for the first time, forced upon us by the successful launch of the Russian Sputnik satellite. We did not have enough science books for each child to have one; so, we scooted the gray metal desks with smooth slanted formica tops together and shared the books that the teacher passed out.

  This year, because there were so many students in the class, we did not have enough history books. On the first day of school, Mrs. Santoro asked if any student could buy the red history book, <u>Great Names in American History.</u> I convinced Mom to go to Superior Office Supply store (where all of the high school students purchased their textbooks each year) and buy the book. I was so proud that I owned the book. I could even underline important information as I studied for tests, and I didn't have to share.

  In fourth grade, Mrs. Santoro required one student each day to memorize a Bible verse and say it to the class each morning. Bobby forgot to memorize a verse one night; so, the next day when it was time to say the verse for the class, he said the shortest verse in the Bible, "Jesus wept." We all laughed, except Mrs. Santoro.

We also said grace as we lined up to go to lunch: "God is great. God is good. Let us thank Him for our food. Amen". We did this every day, and some teachers, like Mrs. Tucker (John's second grade teacher, who also attended our church), read Bible stories after lunch while the students sat at their desks in a darkened classroom with their heads on their folded arms on their desk tops.

Each year we had "health rules" to follow. Each morning we reported to the teacher if we had gone to bed by eight o'clock p. m., brushed our teeth and hair, taken a bath, etc. The teacher punched a "health card" if the "health rules" were followed. We never lied about our health habits, and there were many times that I had to pressure Mom to hurry and roll my freshly washed hair so that I could go to bed before 8:00 p.m.

"Fall of the year" brought "Opening Day" of squirrel hunting season, one of the most important Saturdays in Hemphill, (other than the "Opening Day" of trout season in April.) Soon after that fall day, car antennas would sprout squirrel tails to announce to the world how many squirrels the car owner had bagged thus far. Some cars had only one tail flying in the wind, but others sported four or five tails tied to the length of the antenna, flying horizontally as the car sped up the road.

Dad usually did not tie squirrel tails to the antenna of the black and pink Dodge, but he did often stop in the woods after work and shoot a squirrel or two. He would pull them from the pocket of his hunting jacket and proudly show them to us. They still had a "fur" smell to them. Then, he would cut the tails off and give them to us to show to our friends.

    Dad skinned and cleaned the squirrels and disposed of the hides and entrails in the Tug River, throwing the unwanted parts into the murky water. Then, Mom dipped the delicate cuts of wild meat in flour, fry them, and make gravy. Dad proudly devoured his game, expecting us to do the same.

    "Yeah, boy, this is good squirrel. Nothin' like squirrel gravy on biscuits," he said as he ladled some of the white pasty concoction onto fluffy biscuits.

    I politely tasted a piece that looked like a small chicken thigh, but I could not get the image of the small gray furry creature out of my mind; so, I ate only the biscuits and corn that were served with the squirrel and gravy.

    October was always Fire Prevention Month, a very important time in light of the fact that the Welch School had burned only a few years before. The firemen came to school and gave us red plastic fire hats and "Junior Fire Marshall" badges. We then diligently inspected our homes for pennies in fuse boxes, overloaded outlets, oily rags in closets, and all of the fire hazards we had been warned about. Discussions of fire safety at our house always led to the retelling of a story about a time my oldest brother Tom set the woods on fire in Hemphill.

One summer day back during the War, seven-year-old Tom and his friends Dickie and Wally were playing cowboys and Indians in the woods on the hill above their homes in Orkney Holler. Tom and Dickie tied Wally to a tree, pretending it was a stake, and started a fire with matches Dickie had stolen from the holder behind the coal stove in their kitchen. A breeze caused the fire to spread quickly to the surrounding trees and underbrush. Tom and Dickie got scared and ran home, leaving Wally tied to the tree, surrounded by flames. Tom ran home and hid under the bed in his room. Mom tried to coax him out, but she could not.

Meanwhile, Lenny Hurt, the fire chief of the Blue Blossom Mine in Orkney Hollow, called workers from the mine to fight the fire he had spotted on the hillside. The miners rushed with shovels and hoses, rescued Wally, and quickly put out the fire with water from the nearby creek.

When they questioned Wally about the fire, he told them about Tom and Dickie; so Lenny paid Tom a visit. Mom was at her wits end when she answered the door. Lenny asked to talk to Tom; so Mom escorted him to the bedroom, where he asked Tom why he wouldn't come out from under the bed. Tom told him that he was afraid that they would send him to the reform school at Pruntytown. Lenny assured Tom that he would not be sent to Pruntytown; so Tom came out and promised never to play with matches in the woods and NEVER to tie anyone to a tree again.

October also meant that buckeyes fell from the trees. We peeled the green and brown covering to find the round, smooth nut with the light brown area on it. We made holes in them, strung them together and made necklaces. We carried them in our pockets for good luck, and Dad said that carrying one in your pocket prevented arthritis, which he called Arthur Ritis. (As far as we know, Dad never had arthritis, and he carried a buckeye in his pocket until the day he died.) At the bus stop Hemphill kids always showed up with brown stained fingers and hands in October. We knew that they had peeled the green husk off of black walnuts and laid them out to dry. The stain would not wash off. It just had to "wear off"; so their hands looked dirty for several weeks. Their teachers probably did not punch their "health cards" for many days. It was worth it because when cracked, the walnuts delivered delicious treats that made any cake or batch of fudge delightful.

On Halloween, we made our costumes from whatever was available. I was a princess in one of my older sister Janice's second hand prom dresses. It was yellow with nylon net covering the skirt. (Janice had wired small red artificial roses to the net to try to disguise it from the previous owner who might also attend the prom.) I also wore a black half mask (like Zorro's) made of starched fabric. It was held in place by a thin black elastic band. It was much better than the full-face clown mask that John wore. After trick or treating for only a few minutes, the starched fabric began to "melt" and bleed colors onto his damp lips and sweaty face. At the end of trick or treating on Spruce Street the clown face was wet and contorted around the mouth, where moist lips had yelled, "Trick or treat," as each door opened.

As usual, Mom made molasses popcorn balls as Halloween treats. All day she popped batches of popcorn and boiled a hot molasses and butter mixture on the stove. After pouring the molasses mixture into the large tub of popcorn, she quickly buttered her hands and shaped the balls. She said that the butter kept the molasses from burning her hands. (I thought the butter just made the popcorn balls taste better.) Finally, Mom wrapped the sticky balls in waxed paper and twisted the ends. She proudly placed them in each bag as trick or treaters came to the door, after she returned from "trick or treating" with John and me. Dad gave out the treats while Mom was out with us. That cold Halloween, when we arrived at home, with our coats over our costumes, Dad had a parade of "colored" kids going through the kitchen picking up popcorn balls, getting drinks of water, and being entertained by his funny comments.

Dad often told stories of the "colored" men he worked with at the mines. After that Halloween he told this story:

One time the Coal Company sent me down to Grundy, Virginia, to pick up a motor for the mine. I drove the company truck, and three guys went along to help load the motor. One of the men was a black man named Sam, who rode in the back of the truck with Jim, a white worker. When we got close to Grundy, we covered Sam up with a canvas because we knew that black people were not welcome in Grundy. After loading the equipment, we covered Sam with the canvas and drove out of Buchanan County back to Hemphill.

When the Hemphill mine closed a few months later, I went to Logan County to look for a new job. I returned to the Hemphill mine and told all of the miners that I could probably get them a job at the Sara Ann Mine. Sam said, "I'll follow you anywhere, Mr. Lacy, except to Grundy." After the laughter, he continued, "But I have decided that when I die, I want to be buried in Grundy."

Everyone was puzzled.

"Why?" Dad asked, knowing that people in Grundy would never allow that.

Sam answered with a twinkle in his eye, "Because the devil would never look for a black man in Grundy."

Everyone guffawed, knowing well just what he meant.

CHAPTER 6

In November, 1960, John F. Kennedy was elected President of the United States, and Mom was sure that the Pope would become the dictator of our country very soon. But, on November 11, the focus of all of McDowell County, West Virginia, was the Veteran's Day Parade in downtown Welch. McDowell County had many veterans from World War I, World War II, and the Korean Conflict, and they proudly came to the parade and removed their hats when each flag passed by. It was hard to imagine that only fifteen years before Uncle Buddy, Uncle Donnie and many other Hemphill "boys" had been in the jungles of Guam and other Pacific Islands fighting the Japanese, as well as battling dysentery and malaria. The patriotism still ran strong in their blood. In fact, in 1960, Uncle Buddy bought one of those new-fangled Polaroid Land Cameras that developed black and white pictures right in the camera in sixty seconds. When he excitedly opened the camera to remove the newly developed first picture, he read the words "Made in Japan" on the camera. Enraged that he had spent his hard-earned money on a product of the people he had fought against so hard, he threw the camera to the ground and stomped it into tiny pieces, all the while ranting about "dirty Japs" and crawling around in a coal mine, just to give his money to those sneaky SOB's.

Early morning frost on this Veteran's Day made it necessary to wear coats, hats, and gloves to the ten o'clock a. m. parade. Because parking spaces were so limited, we (Mom, Janice, John, and I) walked the two miles from Hemphill to Welch and stood in a crowd that was two or three deep to watch the bands from the high schools, patriotic floats, local dignitaries and beauty queens in convertibles, and the fire truck with Santa on the back. My favorite part was the prancing majorettes with short skirts, white tasseled calf-high boots with heel and toe taps, and leg makeup that cracked and streaked. Though they twirled batons and marched, what really amazed me was how they could stand the sub-freezing temperatures in such short skirts.

As the parade wound up McDowell Street, we enjoyed each float that honored our country and its military men. The bands played patriotic melodies in much the same vein, but the Kimball High Band (a school for "colored" students) spiritedly strutted past in green and yellow uniforms, sporting the "Kimball Terrors" logo and played a "boogie woogie" tune that I did not know. The Welch High School (Maroon Wave) band was always last, and their majorettes sported white fur berets and short fur-trimmed maroon uniforms. Last, came Santa Claus, and we knew that the parade was over, but the festivities would continue with speeches and the traditional football game that pitted Welch High School Maroon Wave against the archrival

Gary Coaldiggers. After the game, the school with the winning score was presented with a beer barrel, which had been passed between the two schools for as long as anyone could remember. The winning school then painted the wooden keg with the winner's school colors, either Welch's maroon and white, or Gary's red and black. But, as a kid, I cared nothing for this, I just wanted to go home and get warm, after standing in the cold for more than an hour watching the parade. It would be a long walk home, but at least it had warmed up a little when the sun finally topped over the mountains and began to shine full force on Welch.

      Thanksgiving was always a time for family meals and remembrances. Since Mom and Dad were married on Thanksgiving Day in 1935, they always told the story of how they met, courted, and later married.

      It was a May afternoon, sunny and clear. Alice, called Sis by everyone who knew her, and her best friend Ruby decided to walk the three quarters of a mile to the company store in the "Shaft Bottom" section of Hemphill to get a few needed items with scrip. Each car of coal her father loaded underground allowed the family to get scrip, special coins or tokens, to purchase items before payday. Scrip could only be spent at the company store. (Many times a miner would get no pay because all of his pay had already been spent using scrip at the company store.)

Ruby and Sis had gone to the store many times before, but recently, a crew had started road work for the coal company. One of the workers had caught Sis' eye. He was muscular and strong with dark eyes and wavy black hair—a sharp contrast to her own thin frame and blond hair. She knew he was older than her sixteen years, but she wasn't sure how much older.

As they neared the workers, Sis and Ruby began to chatter. As they passed, Sis' eyes met the young man's, and they nodded and spoke, as all Hemphill residents did. Just then, the young man shouted and asked where they were going.

"To the company store," she said with a breathless smile.

His dark eyes lit up when she smiled. "How about getting me some candy bars?" he asked, as he reached into his pocket and handed her a quarter. This was REAL money, not scrip.

She asked, "How many?"

He answered, "Five—two Baby Ruths, an Oh! Henry, and whatever you all want." As he handed her the quarter, her heart leaped as his powerful, albeit dirty, hand brushed her delicate one.

Sis and Ruby walked more rapidly now, with a mission. The needed items were all but forgotten, and they walked straight to the candy counter, getting two Baby Ruths, an Oh! Henry, and two plain Hershey bars for themselves.

Walking quickly toward home, sweets in a brown paper bag, they saw the young man still breaking rocks with a sledge hammer, with his boss Lenny Hurt standing by. As they approached, the young man stopped hammering and waited. Sis removed the two Hershey bars and timidly handed him the bag. He reached into the bag, removed a Baby Ruth and handed it to his boss. She knew then that he was diplomatic and smart. He looked into her eyes and said, "Thank you."

As they walked away, Sis was barely able to contain her leaping spirit. As he watched them go, the young man said to his boss, "I'm going to ask her to go to 'the show' with me."

Lenny stepped back, still chewing his Baby Ruth, and laughed, "That's Tom Bromfield's girl. He'll never let you go out with her."

Well they did go to "the show" at the Pocahontas Theater in Welch. And, as the two young people began to get acquainted, they would find opportunities to meet in Hemphill and talk. One day Sis' sister Tootsie saw them talking near the swinging bridge at Quattrone's Grocery Store. She hurried home to tell her father that Sis was down at the bridge talking to a "Tally", slang for Italian. (She thought he was Italian because the only dark-haired people she knew were of Italian descent.) Her father told Tootsie to go tell Sis to come home right now! "Sagers" don't talk to "Tallies".

The Wednesday before Thanksgiving the young couple went to the Methodist preacher's house in Welch, and the preacher performed the marriage ceremony there. They didn't tell her father (Tom Bromfield) until the next day. There wasn't much he could do about it then.

All three mines in Hemphill had full employment; so all of the company houses were occupied. Even though Lacy worked for the Kingston-Pocahontas Coal Company, there were no vacant houses for the newlyweds. So, they moved into the back bedroom of her father's house. Being winter, it was very cold because the house was heated by one coal stove in the kitchen. Also, the construction of "company houses" was not always substantial. One morning the young couple awoke to snow falling through the ceiling onto their faces. A glass of water placed on a table beside the bed had frozen.

Mom hated winter. She said that she was never warm once "fall of the year" and winter came. They decided that they needed a place of their own, whatever it took.

"What it took" was Lacy's pride and joy, a red 1933 Chevy Roadster. Lacy had heard that Eddie Mason's wife had left him and gone to live with her family in Kentucky. Eddie wanted to follow her there, but he had no transportation. Lacy made a deal: If Eddie would convince the coal company to let him rent Eddie's house, Lacy would give Eddie the beloved Roadster.

The deal was struck, and the young couple moved into Eddie's small house. When they entered their first house, it was apparent that Eddie's wife had left in a fit of anger. The sink contained greasy, cold fried chicken, where she had thrown it during her last shouting match with Eddie. Sis and Lacy just laughed, cleaned up the mess, and enjoyed all of their new belongings that came with the house—furniture, dishes, pots and pans, linens, even a "slop jar" and catalogs in the outhouse. They had finally "gone to housekeeping!"

  That house brought many good times to Sis and Lacy. The first baby Tom was delivered there by Dr. Anderson. Visitors were always welcome there. Almost weekly, hobos would hop off the train in Hemphill and knock on Sis's door. They were always looking for work, like mowing, cleaning up, or painting. She had no work for them. However, she always fed them a hearty breakfast of eggs, bacon or ham and toast or leftover biscuits. One day she asked Lacy in a puzzled tone, "Why do the hobos stop here, and not at the neighbors' houses?"

  Lacy laughed, "They hop off the train when it slows down to deliver sand to the sand house just down the road. They can sleep pretty good in the sand pile, and they play cards to pass the time until the next train comes. They spread the word about who cooks the best grub, and they look for marks made by hobos who have come here before. Our gate has a "hobo mark" on it; so they know you will feed them."

Mom felt a little embarrassed that she was so naïve, but she did not remove the mark from the gate.

During the first years of marriage in that first house, each payday Sis and Lacy went to Quattrone's and bought five chickens and a quart of oysters and took them to her sister Tootsie, who still lived with her husband in her father's house. She fried the chickens on Sunday and made oyster stew. The whole family, including Papaw and the younguns' feasted on the delicacies. After the kitchen was cleaned up, local musicians (fiddlers and banjo pickers) showed up. Most of them were young single miners who "boarded" with coal miners' families, paying five dollars a month for a room and meals. Some of them lived in the coal company's "boardin' house" at the head of Warwick Holler. All of them played "by ear".

"If you hum it, I'll figger out how it goes," they'd say, when asked to play a tune they did not know.

The kids were put in one bed in the back bedroom, and the young couples danced into the night. The next morning the "paint" was worn off the linoleum floors. The coal camp houses had that cheap painted tarpaper linoleum to cover gray washed board floors. Tootsie and Papaw didn't care. The coal company would replace the linoleum soon anyway.

Thanksgiving, 1960, was a dreary, cool day. The green leaves of summer that gave the mountains around Hemphill a soft, even fluffy, appearance were gone. The mountains were stark and black, covered by naked black tree trunks and branches. As I looked out the living room window at the small white houses with coal dirt yards across the river, I heard the sharp sound of a gun and the high-pitched screech of a hurt animal. I ran to ask Mom about the terrifying sound.

She grinned and said, "Thanksgiving is hog-killin' time. See the pens up on the hill? The colored folks are killing a hog so they can have ham and bacon for the winter."

She continued, "We always killed a hog every Thanksgiving when my father was alive. Then, we salted and cured the meat. It was really good, but I was always too squeamish to ever actually participate in the killing."

One Thanksgiving, my father, who we called Pawpaw, my brothers, and Lacy killed a hog on the hill above the house. They worked all day up on the hill, scraping the hair off the hog, cutting up the hams and "side meat", and boiling renderings. They had a few jars of "white lightning" up there, and the longer they worked, the more they drank. When it was finally time to carry the valuable meat back to the house, they were all tired and tipsy. As Papaw picked up the largest hams, he dropped them into the pile of scrapings and hair. He continued to drop and drag the hams all the way to the house. They were a mess, but *meat was too valuable during those hard times. We just washed them off and ate the ham anyway.*

I was amazed and a little ashamed to know that my relatives were so "hard up". I didn't really understand "hard times", but I was glad we were having turkey for our Thanksgiving dinner. The smells of the celery and onion for the dressing, and the rising yeast rolls comforted me.

After Mom had cooked all morning, it was finally time for the long awaited dinner. The adults sat down at the dining room table and the kids sat at the child-sized table and chairs that had been used for tea parties only the day before. As we all told how delicious everything tasted, especially the turkey, Dad began to tell about one unusual Thanksgiving dinner during the early years of their marriage.

Mom and her sister Tootsie walked from Hemphill to the Pocahontas Theater in Welch the day before Thanksgiving to see a movie. After the show, as usual, there was a drawing for a prize. The prizes were usually pink glassware or some household item, but on this night the prize was a large, live Tom Turkey.

When the winner was announced, it was Tootsie. She was so "tickled" as she went up to claim her prize. They handed her a large live bird, and she and Mom walked out of the theater and down McDowell Street (Welch's main road), with the turkey securely tucked under her arm. Folks stopped and stared, and kids pointed at the thin young lady with a large turkey under her tiring arm, but the prize winners kept on walking the two miles to Hemphill. At times the turkey got restless and tried to squirm to get free, but Tootsie held her prize firmly under her arm and strutted proudly home.

Once at home, she immediately wrung the bird's neck, and put him in boiling water to loosen the feathers. She worked all night plucking, washing, plucking, washing, and finally plucking the "pin feathers" out of the bird's skin. In order to have the turkey ready for Thanksgiving dinner, she had to put coal in the stove and start to bake the bird about four o'clock in the morning. (Meanwhile, Sis had gone to bed. After all, SHE didn't win a turkey.)

By afternoon when the turkey was served, everyone said it was the best turkey they had ever eaten. However, Tootsie went straight to bed, leaving Sis to wash the dishes and clean up the leftovers.

Everyone laughed at the much-told story, and then we relaxed or played all afternoon. As it got dark that evening, I again looked out the window at the houses in "colored camp". I saw people standing under a light with head coverings on. I shouted, "Look, it's a manger scene. They are already celebrating Christmas."

Mom, Dad, and John rushed to the window, and Mom and Dad began to laugh. "That's not a manger scene. Those people are still cutting up that hog they killed this morning. They have the parts laid out on a table under the big light, and their heads are covered to keep hair from getting in the meat."

    It still looked like a manger scene to me. After all, Thanksgiving was over, and Christmas was on the way!

CHAPTER 7

"Now that Thanksgiving has passed," Mrs. Santoro stood at the front of the classroom and told us, "it is time to think about Christmas. For this month, all of the Bible verses that you memorize should be about the birth of Jesus."

"Also," she continued, "we will draw names, and you should buy a gift with a fifty cent price limit for the student whose name you draw."

I was so excited. It was one of my favorite things about Christmas in school. I cautiously reached into a bag that Mrs. Santoro passed around the class and pulled out a folded slip of paper and checked to be sure MY own name was not on my slip. This year I got Harold's name. He sat right in front of me, and he was the best artist in the class, and I knew exactly what kind of gift he would like. I secretly hoped that some rich kid from Welch got my name so that I would get a great gift, like the one I was going to buy for Harold.

On Saturday, Dad drove Mom, John, and me to Welch in the pink and black Dodge. The wet streets were turned into a mini lake of black water when the coal dust mixed with rain. He dropped us off in front of G. C. Murphy's. As we got out of the car, we heard a blast of music from the temporary hut set up by the Salvation Army beside the Flat Iron Drug Store and the tinkling of a bell being rung by the Lion's Club members who had volunteered to ring the bell on that day. We walked slowly so the slimy black mud would not splash onto the backs of our legs as we walked, and we were careful to stay as far away from the street as possible to avoid being splashed by passing cars.

    We stepped from the messy sidewalk into a bustling world of shopping delights. We were immediately greeted by the sights and scents of the candy counter whose tall glass cases contained chocolate covered peanuts, small Clark bars, jellied orange slices, vanilla filled chocolate drops, and peppermints for Christmas. The most special smell came from the roasting peanuts which were stirred by an automatic contraption. This day, there was a sign on the peanut case, which read "A lucky coin may be in any bag of nuts!" There were pennies, nickels, dimes, and even quarters dispersed throughout the glass case of nuts, and a coin might be scooped into any bag that was purchased. I was hoping Dad would get a big coin in his bag of "television peanuts" today.

    Before we left the house, Mom had handed John and me a dollar and fifty cents each for Christmas shopping—fifty cents for our "name gifts" at school, and a dollar to buy gifts for Mom and Dad. John and I told Mom we were going to the toy department in the back right corner of the store, but we secretly went down the wide marble stairs with wrought iron and wood banisters to the housewares department. I selected dish cloths for Mom. Then we went back up the stairs, where John looked at the perfume--Blue Waltz, Evening in Paris, and others. He chose Evening in Paris. We had very little left for Dad's gifts; so, John bought him a new handkerchief, and I bought him a five-inch tall pink artificial Christmas tree. I knew it was not really an appropriate gift for Dad, but I just could not think about a man's gift with all of the stimulation from the sights, smells and sounds of Christmas that seemed to whir around me.

Finally, John and I hurried to the toy department. This time I wasn't looking at dolls and toy kitchen utensils. I wanted to buy a long tin box of water color paints with a brush. I was disappointed that it only cost twenty-nine cents; so I bought a box of sixteen crayons to go with the paint set for Harold.

John was looking at paddle balls and yo-yos, but he finally decided on a model airplane for his "name gift". It was forty-nine cents, plus tax, but he had a few cents left from his dollar for Mom's and Dad's gifts. We were "pleased as punch" with our purchases (except for the small brush-like Christmas tree), and we secretly held our bags as we met Mom at the front of the store.

A few minutes later Dad wandered up. He was holding four small white bags, and one red and white striped one, and I knew we would have "television candy and nuts" again tonight.

"Where have you been?" asked Mom.

"Well, it took me a while to find a place to park," he answered. "I had to park up by the bank. Then, I saw George from the Capitol, and I stopped and talked to him."

"You didn't go in that beer joint, did you?" she accused.

He grinned and answered, "No, I've been looking at housecoats so I could buy you one for Christmas. But, they haven't marked them down enough yet. I need to wait until Christmas Eve, after all of those fat women have tried them on and drug them on the floor. Then, they will mark them down enough for me."

Mom just shook her head. We waited in front of Murphy's while Dad went and got the car, circled around on Welch's two one-way streets, and stopped to pick us up. We headed back to Spruce Street. Later that week we came back to Welch at night to see the lights. Strings of colored lights criss-crossed the two one-way streets, and flashing red bells greeted us at the entrance to the business section of town. Then, we went to Stewart Street to see the decorations on the houses there. They sure were different from the few pitiful strings of lights at a few houses in Hemphill. The houses on Stewart Street had green wreaths on the doors, lighted pine trees in the yards, and bright lights circling the doors and windows.

The week before Christmas Dad went to the "woods" near the mines and cut down a Christmas tree. He brought it home after work, sticking out of the trunk of the car. This year the tree had the usual bare spot that we put against the wall, but it also had lots of bare spots that needed limbs cut from the bottom of the tree and taped to the trunk with black electrical tape. The large colored lights (some of them were shaped like bells and Santa) and the bubble lights made it the most beautiful tree ever. I stared intently at the colored balls, each one different and special. There was even a "wartime" ball, made of red transparent celluloid with a string connected to it with paper instead of metal. John and I helped put the aluminum icicles on, placing each strand on separately and carefully. As Mom put the white sheet under the decorated tree, we knew that gifts would soon appear.

    The next day, we got a large box from Aunt Ethel at the post office. It contained a package for each of us. We anxiously awaited the day we could open the bright and secret packages.

    The Sunday before Christmas at church, each person attending got a box of hard Christmas candy with a string handle. I was very careful not to drop the box on the tiled floor because it would fly open and the candy would make popping sounds as it went all over the floor, maybe even up to the pulpit, where the preacher stood. I just couldn't resist opening the box and putting a piece of wintergreen ribbon candy in my mouth. I savored the fresh taste; then, I popped a raspberry shaped piece into my mouth. It was filled with a sweet gooey jelly in the middle. I carefully closed the box and saved the rest. I knew that when we got home, Mom would put her candy in a dish on the coffee table, and within a day or two, all of the pieces would stick together and be impossible to separate.

     Lily Neil stopped John and me as we left church and said that she had heard Sam Sidote read a letter to Santa Claus from John on Radio Station WELC. John was too young to write a letter; so he dictated one to our older sister Janice, and it was read aloud on the radio, along with hundreds of others written by hopeful coalfield children. John felt like surely Santa would bring what he wanted if Sam Sidote had read his letter for everyone, even Santa, to hear.

     The week before Christmas at school, we made cards for our parents and ornaments for our trees, but the last day before Christmas vacation, we had a party and revealed whose name we had drawn. Harold opened his paints and crayons, and I could see that he really liked my gift and that he was surprised that I had kept it a secret. I anxiously opened my gift from Charlotte, who had drawn my name. It was a book, <u>The Bobbsey Twins at the Seashore.</u> I was a little disappointed because it seemed such a long hard book, but I told her that I liked it and that I couldn't wait to read it.

     At the close of the day, Mrs. Santoro opened the gift that each student had brought to school for her. I gave her hand lotion, and she put it on right in class and talked about how good it smelled. Then, we excitedly rode Bus 59 home, ready for Christmas.

Since Christmas was on Sunday this year, we had an outdoor nativity scene at the church on Stewart Street on Thursday and Friday night before Christmas. We had practiced after school for weeks, and everyone was ready. I was an angel; so I had to hide behind the bushes and appear after the "Angel of the Lord" climbed up the ladder to the top of the stable and lifted her arms as the tape played these words: "And suddenly there was with the angel a multitude of the heavenly host praising God and saying, 'Glory to God in the highest and on earth peace, good will toward men.'"

It was dark and cold behind the bushes as we sat on blankets through the appearance of Mary and Joseph at the inn and the shepherds in the fields (side yard of the church). Then as Nancy, the Angel of the Lord, climbed the ladder behind the stable and got to the top, she tripped on the long robe and fell from the ladder. The tape kept going, and we appeared on cue without the Angel of the Lord, singing "Glory to God in the highest…" The preacher heard the ladder fall (it wasn't quiet), and helped Nancy up. She was shaken up, but well enough to meet us in the fellowship hall after the play and enjoy hot chocolate with marshmallows and cookies.

Just before Christmas, Quattrone's Grocery was busy selling special items to their Italian customers. The store was bustling with customers, and strange new odors of special fish greeted each one. There were also candy coated almonds, only available at Christmas. Dante delivered our Christmas needs in his pickup truck—baking needs, and punch ingredients. As always, he brought us a box of Candy Cupboard chocolates, a gift for loyal customers.

We didn't buy a turkey or ham at Quattrone's because the coal company always gave Dad a turkey and a ham at Christmas. He went to the company store and got the treasured meats, as well as the company and union "treats". Each family member received a brown paper bag with an orange, an apple, a candy bar, a pack of gum, a candy cane, and some loose nuts in the shell. The union treat always had bigger and better candy bars than the company treat. The nuts always filled the round, bark-covered wooden bowl with a metal nutcracker reminding me of pliers in the center, and sometimes the fruit and candy canes appeared in our stockings on Christmas morning.

We opened gifts under the tree on Christmas Eve. Aunt Ethel's gifts were always first. I got a box of lace handkerchiefs from my dad's sister. Janice, my older sister, got a chocolate torte (we didn't even know what a torte was), and John got a small Mickey Mouse rubber inner tube for swimming. I think Aunt Ethel thought John was three years old, instead of six. Besides, we couldn't swim in Hemphill, especially not in the winter.

After opening gifts, John and I went to bed and waited for Santa. On this night we slept together in the big iron bed in John's room. I always slept with Janice in a double bed in her room, but tonight Mom suggested that we sleep in John's room. That way, we could get up at the same time on Christmas morning.

As I lay in bed, listening for Santa, I heard scraping, and whispers, and grunts. Thinking it might be Santa, I opened my eyes and saw Dad and Mom lifting and pushing the small roll-top desk (that had been in Janice's room) down the steps. They were grunting and shushing, and I was confused.

When I awoke at six o'clock in the morning, I no longer believed in Santa Claus. Beside the tree sat the roll top desk from Janice's room. With it was a small metal globe, a small, but heavy, maroon metal sewing machine, and a Betsy McCall doll. The desk and sewing machine were not new. It was then that I understood about Santa because Santa had not been known to deliver used toys. On the other hand, "Santa" answered John's letter, delivering a large box of plastic "Wagon Train" figures, complete with wagons, horses, cowboys with lassos, Indians, and Ward Bond, the leader of the Wagon Train, himself. He also got a fire truck, and all of his toys were NEW.

After Christmas dinner, we went to visit Aunt Anna Belle and Uncle Buddy and the cousins. We wanted to see what Santa had brought them for Christmas. My cousin Connie had a new life-size doll. It was terrific! She had a new toy kitchen too. All of the cousins had really nice presents, and there were no used toys in their piles of gifts. I took my Betsy McCall doll to show to Connie, but I did not tell her about the desk or sewing machine. This time I did not feel sorry for my cousins. I was envious.

    On Christmas evening, Mom got out the punch bowl, and we made the traditional Christmas punch. Each family member added a special ingredient: ginger ale and strawberry "pop" in large glass bottles called "Party Paks", double-strength tea, lemon juice, etc.

    Mom put in the frozen strawberries (picked last summer) and orange sherbet. My older brother Ron was the official taster, and after he gave his official approval, Mom ladled the foamy pink liquid into the small crystal cups. Later that night, Ron said that the punch gave him indigestion, and he needed an Alka-Seltzer. Dad said, "Next year we'll put the Alka-Seltzer right in the punch for you."

    At last it was time to tell the "locket story". On Christmas Mom wore her gold and black enameled book-shaped locket which revealed pictures of Dad and her when opened. I asked her to tell us about their first Christmas as newlyweds. She began the traditional story.

    We were living with Papaw, my father, and we didn't have much money. I couldn't buy anything for Lacy, but he gave me a small box on Christmas Eve. When I opened it, there was this locket. I was thrilled with such a special gift.

My sister Tootsie and her husband Archie were at Papaw's house for Christmas Eve too, and when Archie saw that Lacy had bought me such a nice gift, he felt really bad. He had not bought Tootsie a gift at all. Well, he asked Lacy to take him up to Welch to get Tootsie a locket too.

"It's almost eight o'clock at night. No stores will be open." Lacy said. But, Archie persisted, and they drove the two miles to Welch.

It was easy to find a parking space because all of the stores were closed, but Archie insisted that they check U.S. Jewelers, where Lacy had bought the locket. As they approached the door, a light was visible in the back of the store. They knocked loudly on the door until a man came to the door and opened it. He was the owner of the store, and he listened to Archie's plea for a locket. He eagerly sold him a necklace, much like Sis's, and Archie left the store a happy husband. They later learned that the owner of the store was Jewish, and since he did not celebrate Christmas, he was working late at the store.

Christmas had come and gone in 1960. Little did I know that it would be our last Christmas on Spruce Street.

Icicles

CHAPTER 8

Each new year in Hemphill was marked by the arrival of the new calendar from Angelo's Barber Shop with the words, "Same barber, same location since 1935" on it. However, 1961 was different. It arrived with a real bang—literally. Beginning in the late afternoon on New Year's Eve, Hemphill residents began setting off firecrackers and firing shotguns in celebration. Just before midnight my Uncle Buddy attached dynamite (from the Trailee Mine where he worked) to the clothesline stretched across his front yard on a pulley. At precisely 12:00 midnight, he lit the dynamite and wheeled the pulley to push it away from the front porch. It made a great explosion all right, but the blast tore the clothesline from the pulley. Buddy spent New Year's Day reattaching the line to the pulley so that Anna Belle could hang out the laundry for those six kids, including diapers for the baby. When he heard about the escapade, Dad laughed and said that Buddy must have visited the "coal miners' drug store" on New Year's Eve. (That was his code name for the liquor store.)

"Blue cold" is what Dad called those days in January and February that were so cold that it hurt to breathe in the frigid air. We looked out the window at Tug River and saw that ice was spreading from each bank, attempting to meet in the middle. Every puddle was frozen, and stayed frozen for days. Two or three foot long icicles hung from the roofs of the houses, waiting for a thaw to drop on unsuspecting passersby. The houses in Hemphill were heated by burning coal, either in a furnace for the whole house or in coal stoves placed in certain rooms. Coal was delivered to our house by a big truck from Page Coal and Coke Company, where Dad worked. A man drove up to the house and shoveled the coal into a small window in the basement. We were lucky at our house because we had a stoker, a machine that was filled with coal once a day and then steadily fed the coal to the furnace. Before we had a stoker, Dad or Mom had to shovel coal into the fire every couple of hours. Dad removed the ashes from the lower chamber of the furnace after the smoldering gray powdery fragments had dropped down onto the basement floor. When they had cooled, Dad carried the ashes to the garden to fertilize the soil for spring planting.

We could sit on the wooden radiator covers and get warm and watch the river flowing by, remembering the big flood of 1957, when many of the houses across the river in "colored camp" had murky river water past the windows. The radiators were a perfect place to dry our woolen mittens and scarves in an effort to remove the "wet wool" smell from them, so we could wear them tomorrow, and the next day, and the next...The "dead of winter" was often the time that we were reminded of the fire safety lessons we had been taught in October. Often when Mom opened the heavy iron furnace door, revealing the dancing flames, she would warn me to stay back, though I was tempted to get close and warm my hands. She often told the story of the little girl in Hemphill who backed up to a fireplace to warm herself. Suddenly the flames lapped at the hem of her dress, and she was immediately wrapped in flame, screaming and running, hair and clothes fueling the flames. Once the flames were extinguished, she lingered in pain for a few days, then died in agony.

"You know how it hurts when you burn your finger on the stove? Well, think of that pain all over your body," Mom said emphatically. After each lecture, I was not tempted to get too close to an open flame. I also thought of that tortured little girl every time the preacher talked about hell, and I was determined not to burn there.

No matter how cold it got, life went on in Hemphill. Mom washed clothes and hung them out on lines, propped up with poles to keep the clothes from weighing the lines down and dragging on the ground. It was a cold, miserable job to pin the heavy wet clothes to the line. They often froze stiff before they dried and were impossible to fold until they were warmed on the radiators. Towels were stiff and scratchy in the winter from drying on the line.

Work and school continued as normal, even in sub-zero temperatures. George Bryson was the Superintendent of the McDowell County Schools, and he believed that school should never be closed for any reason. He once said, "Even if students have to go to school in a submarine, school will not be cancelled." So, I went to school on those "blue cold" days, bundled up with wool coat, red rubber boots over my shoes, two pairs of gloves or mittens, and a wool scarf that covered my head and ears and wrapped around my neck and covered my mouth. The scarf got wet within minutes from the moisture from my mouth, but it was better than not having it there. In mid-January I even wore corduroy pants under my dress for warmth, but they had to be removed when I got to school because girls did not wear pants to school—ever.

In the middle of January, 1961, we awoke to temperatures of twelve degrees below zero. John and I bundled up and walked around the curve, past the church steps, up the hill to the "county road" toward the school bus stop with Debbie and Cathy, my friends who lived up the street. It was more than a half a mile, and we could hardly move, much less walk and carry a lunchbox, with all of the clothing on. When we got to the bus stop, most of the other kids from the other sections of Hemphill were already there. Some of the first graders were crying from the cold, and the tears were freezing on their faces. Some of them had really runny noses, with thick mucous streaks between their noses and mouths that Dad called "lamb's legs". Everyone was jumping around and complaining. It soon became apparent that the bus was late. The safety patrol said, "Maybe the bus ain't comin', and we should go home."

Roselle replied, "There hain't no such word as ain't." We all laughed quietly under our scarves, not willing to engage Roselle in a disagreement. It would probably get violent. It usually did when she was involved.

We waited and waited for what seemed like hours. Finally, we heard the "blee, blee, blee" of the chains on the bus tires. (The sound reminded me of the merry tune played at the beginning of the Captain Kangaroo television show.) The bus was about forty-five minutes late. Mr. Day, the driver, said that he had trouble getting the big yellow bus started. It felt good to sit down and be out of the cold air, but the heater on the bus was no match for twelve degrees below zero.

When we got to Welch Elementary School on Stewart Street, there were very few students there. Some of the buses did not run at all, and most of the town kids were absent that day. Mrs. Santoro let me put my hands on the radiator beside the window. It took several minutes to get some feeling back into my fingers. When we left school, the sun had come out, but puddles and icicles still remained frozen, as did much of Tug River.

Spruce Street was great for sledding in the winter. Every street and yard was a hill. We had an old sled that we could ride down the hill, with two or three kids stacked on top of each other. It had a cross-piece of wood attached to the front for guiding it. We had to be careful not to run in front of moving cars or into the river. So we always posted a lookout who would yell "Car" when a car was coming into our path.

The sled was dangerous enough in those conditions, but that winter Dad found the round metal top from an old water heater, and we commandeered it for sledding. Not only was it fast, but it was uncontrollable, once it started going downhill. On its inaugural ride, John started down the hill on the disc, laughing and yelling, only to realize, he had no way to stop it. He went straight over the river bank, broke through the ice, and landed in the murky water of Tug River. Luckily, the water was only about ten inches deep. He dragged the disk back up the bank and went home to take a warm bath, dry off, and change out of the blackened, sewage-soaked clothes. After the initial scare, we laughed and laughed, but I was never brave enough to try to ride the metal disk.

It got dark early in January and February; so in order to continue the sleigh riding fun, some of the teenagers built a fire of old tires and wood. It was a way to keep warm, albeit smelly, and to extend the sledding fun. Toward the end of the evening, when it was time to go home, some older boys, riding a scrounged up trunk from a 1948 Dodge, sledded right through the fire. That sent sparks flying and kids running, and those boys laughed all the way home.

A special treat on snowy days was "snow cream". My older sister Janice always insisted on making ice cream from freshly fallen snow. We waited until the snow was several inches deep, and then ran outside and scooped up a large bowlful. We always used freshly fallen snow because after just a few hours snow in Hemphill became covered with the gray dust that seemed to permeate everything in the coal camp. And, we were careful to gather clean snow because everyone knew "you can't eat yellow snow", referring to the yellow stain that dog (or other) urine leaves in the snow.

After retrieving the fluffy white snow, Janice added a little Carnation cream, some sugar, and some vanilla, and we all enjoyed "ice cream". It was rare to have ice cream in the winter, but snowy days made a good excuse.

Winter seemed to be the time of sickness. Measles was one of the dreaded diseases that I came down with in the winter of 1961. I had already had the three-day measles (rubella), but now I had the "big measles", with red splotches all over my arms, legs, chest, and back. The spots were not really large; so I think they called them "big measles" because they lasted longer than the three-day kind. I lay on the couch far from the RCA floor model television, hardly able to see the small rounded screen with "Boston Blackie" and "Sergeant Preston of the Yukon" emblazoned in black and white images. When Dad came home, he had a pair of wire rimmed men's sunglasses in his hand. He gingerly put them on my eyes, saying, "You can go blind with the measles." I got really scared, but not scared enough to wear those sunglasses and miss seeing "Scoop and Snoop" and their cartoons.

I missed ten days of school with the measles, and one thawing afternoon, Debbie, my friend from up the street, knocked on the front door. Mom led her to the couch, and she had some books and worksheets from Mrs. Santoro. Then she handed me a pack of multi-colored Lifesavers. She said they were from

Norman, and that he was asking how I was. Before the measles, Norman had been bringing me a pack of Lifesavers every day, and so I guess he was continuing the tradition. I thanked her for delivering the candy, but not for the homework, and she went on her way.

      As I recovered from the measles, John came down with a sore throat. After trying honey and lemon and Smith Brothers Cough Drops, Mom took him to Dr. Anderson. She bundled him up, and they walked up Spruce Street, around the curve, down the stone church steps, past Stafford's Grocery Store, across the big iron bridge to the first house in "colored camp." They stepped up onto the small porch and entered the small white frame house. There was a small waiting area that was empty that day. The old doctor stepped out of his examining room and asked them to come in. As John sat on the examining table, the doctor said, "Say Ahhh," as he pressed John's tongue with the wide wooden tongue depressor. He told Mom, the sore throat was just a result of a cold, and he proceeded to dip a long cotton swab in a reddish liquid. He then brushed the swab along the back of John's throat, thus "painting" it. Then, he put a dozen or so small pills, green, yellow, pink, black and white, into a small brown envelope and told Mom that John should take one of each for three days. Mom paid Dr. Anderson three dollars for the visit and the pills, and she and John walked home, both feeling better.

When I got home from school, John told me about his visit to Dr. Anderson and showed me his envelope of tiny pills. I asked Mom why she took John to Dr. Anderson, since I had never been to him. Mom said that she was worried about John's throat, and since she didn't think he should go all the way to Grace Hospital in Welch on the city bus, they just walked over to Dr. Anderson's office.

I asked Mom who was this old Dr. Anderson, and why was his office in "colored camp". I had seen him drive his big black Cadillac slowly through Hemphill, but I did not know that he was "colored". Mom laughed and said that Dr. Anderson was white. His office was located in "colored camp" because that was a central location for all of the coal mines in Hemphill. I was confused. What did coal mines have to do with Dr. Anderson? She explained:

Dr. James Howard Anderson was the Coal Company doctor in Hemphill when I was a little girl. He came here before I was born in 1918, and he delivered almost every baby in Hemphill for decades, including your two older brothers and your sister, who were born at home. He was educated at Harvard, and when he came here his office was the first company house in "colored" camp. It has been there ever since. In those days, doctors made "house calls", and he walked to see patients in the coal camp, even though he was given a horse by the coal company. It was just easier to walk up the hills and rutted roads than to ride. He delivered every coal miner's baby for years. If the mother had not chosen a name for her new boy baby, Dr. Anderson always named him James or Howard (his names). So, expectant mothers in Hemphill soon learned to have names chosen before the baby was due if they did not like the names James or Howard.

Dr. Anderson always brought a rubber sheet to protect bedding when he delivered a baby, and it was expected that the sheet be washed and returned to his office the next day. He was kind and efficient in his duty, but he was not particularly compassionate toward unwed mothers. He told one young girl who was crying loudly during labor, "Be quiet. You weren't crying and yelling when you got this baby."

Dr. Anderson was also expected to treat all work related injuries for coal miners, including serious mine accidents. He often went with injured miners to the Welch Emergency Hospital if their injuries were too serious for his expertise or limited equipment.

Dr. Anderson is a part of our Hemphill heritage. He used to live right here on Spruce Street, but he moved to Welch when the mines shut down. He is someone to be respected and admired, and even though he is no longer employed by the coal company, he keeps office hours here in Hemphill for those who need him.

Besides Dr. Anderson, there were other trusted doctors in the area; however, most ailments were treated with home remedies, like warm sweet oil for earaches, warm water enemas for stomach aches, and a salt water gargle for sore throats. There were also over the counter medicines, such as Vick's Salve for a chest cold, but if the sickness became severe, some doctors, such as Dr. Linkous in Welch made house calls. One time Mom had the flu, and she was not able to get out of bed to visit a doctor. So, kindly Dr. Linkous drove to Hemphill with his black leather bag and stethoscope, checked Mom over and prescribed some medicines. Dad had to drive to the Flat Iron Drugstore in Welch to get the prescriptions filled, and he brought the pills and cough medicine home in small brown glass bottles.

     Dreary winter monotony in Hemphill was interrupted by several cheerful venders who came to Spruce Street from time to time. The Jewel Tea Man might deliver dishes, soaps, or even tea to Mrs. Henderson. Ti-Ti Legato drove the red paneled Peerless Laundry truck. At least once during the winter Mom would send the wool coats and skirts (that we had worn for two months now) to be cleaned. Ti-Ti would return them with a smile and a happy greeting. He was a real celebrity on Spruce Street. The "Tinker Man" drove a blue paneled truck that had several tools, wires, and pans hanging from the side. He usually stopped at the Jones' house to repair small appliances for Mrs. Jones.

     "Stopper" Wilson, a full-time coal miner, part-time Methodist preacher and TV repairman came to our house whenever the round-screened black and white floor model television needed a new tube. "Stopper" worked with Dad at the Black Wolf Mine near Gary, and if our TV developed rolling or narrowing of the picture, he would come to fix it on Saturday or after work on weekdays. It usually did not take long to fix the TV, since he carried a supply of cylindrical glass tubes in his truck.

     The "Leatherwood Man" delivered milk three days a week to the houses on Spruce Street. Mom would leave a note for the milkman telling him how many half gallon waxy cardboard cartons of milk she needed. She might also ask for buttermilk or butter to be delivered. She always included cash with the note that was left on the front porch. When we woke up, the requested items would be sitting on the front porch. In the winter, the temperatures kept the milk cold but, hopefully, not frozen.

     This winter, the Leatherwood Dairy had a special offer. The paper that was left with the milk on the front porch announced that a free "popgun" was available in exchange for twenty-five seals from Leatherwood products. John was so excited. Each week he carefully cut the circular seals off the waxy cartons and saved them. After eight weeks, Janice helped John send the seals in to the company. John waited every day for the arrival of his "popgun", and he made plans to play cowboys with Larry and do target shooting with empty cans.

Then one day, I brought a brown envelope from the post office. It as addressed to John. He warily opened it to find a flimsy cardboard gun-shaped cut-out with folded paper in the barrel. When it was held and flipped forward, the paper popped out and made a popping sound. This was just like the paper poppers that the kids at school made every day (unbeknownst to the teachers, of course). John was so disappointed that he put the "popgun" in a drawer, and I never saw him play with it. We all learned something about the power of advertising to make things seem better than they really were.

CHAPTER 9

As always, March, 1961, in Hemphill was a "deceptive month". It was the first mostly-sunny month since October, but the cold temperatures and biting wind would "cut right through you", if you were outside for very long. We still wore our coats, scarves, and gloves most days, but the galoshes were less used now. In 1961 no one wore tennis shoes, or sneakers, unless he was involved in a basketball game or other sport—no one except our neighbor, Bobby Joe Cooper. We thought it was quite humorous that he wore sneakers all the time, even to school. Even more comical to us was the fact that he didn't walk, like most kids. He "danced" everywhere he went in his black Chuck Taylor All-Star shoes. When we saw him "dancing" up Spruce Street one evening, Dad said, "There's Bobby Joe; I ain't laid eyes on him all winter. Look at 'im; he's so dumb, he's happy." Then we all laughed, but secretly I admired the dark-eyed fashion rebel from down the street.

In February, Dad took out the seed catalogs that had been coming in the mail since Christmas and looked for the "almanac" to plan his spring garden planting. He always said that you need to plant a garden every year to prepare for the "Hoover Times" that he believed would surely come again. Having lived through the hard times of the Great Depression, he felt that he should always be prepared. So, he used the "signs" in the almanac to plan when he should plant each vegetable. Onions, potatoes, and other root crops were planted when the "signs" were in the feet; otherwise, they would bear only leaves. Cabbage and tomatoes were planted when the "signs" were in the head, or they would not bear well. It all seemed very scientific, and it usually worked for Dad.

During the cold days near the end of February, Dad announced, "The sap's risin' in the maple trees. Reminds me of the time when I was a boy about twelve and decided to make me some maple candy."

I was livin' with my married sister Stella, since my mother had been killed in a car wreck in 1924. (On a Sunday drive, the car overturned and my sister and me climbed out of the ripped canvas top in the back.) Anyway, Stella made sure I had something to eat and clean clothes, but I never had any candy or sweets, 'cept maybe jelly. So, when the sap started to rise in the maple trees, I decided to make me some maple candy.

I got up early one cold Saturday morning and chopped wood (about a cord.) That took a few hours. Then I got the small bucket of sap that had I had hung on the maple tree in the woods in our house. I built a fire with that wood and began to boil the liquid sap. I added wood and stirred and stirred and stirred and boiled and boiled and boiled. About sunset the sap had boiled down to a hardened piece of maple sweetness about the size of half dollar. I was dog tired, but I took that candy home and wrapped it in paper. I wouldn't tell anybody about it, and every once in a while, I'd sneak it out of my pocket and take a lick from it. It was the best candy I've ever had.

Now, I understood why "television candy" was so important to Dad every Saturday.

With the first week in March came my older sister's birthday on the seventh and my younger brother's birthday on the eighth. It was the family joke that Janice always got a red velvet cake for her birthday, and John always got a half of a red velvet cake that was left over from the day before. This year, however, John (and I) got something really special for his birthday. Dad took us to the Pocahontas Theater in Welch to see our first big screen movie. We were very excited and were sure to be bathed, dressed and ready that evening when Dad said it was time to go. We quietly rode in the pink and black Dodge up Spruce Street, around the "county road", past Welch Emergency Hospital, stopping at the stop light at the mouth of Brown's Creek. Our anticipation mounted as we rode up the main street in Welch toward the theater, which was located on the far end of town. We hoped that we would not be late and miss any of our first movie, when the most dreaded obstacle to Welch traffic appeared. The crossing gate at the train tracks in the middle of town began descending as we looked up the street. All cars stopped and waited as a long Norfolk and Western train crawled across the street in front of us. The Norfolk and Western passenger train was moving very slowly because it had just left the train station and was slow to accelerate through town.

"That's the Powhatan Arrow," said Dad. "See, the maroon bullet-shaped locomotive has the name on it in gold letters. Just last year, the N & W Railroad stopped using steam engines and changed to all diesel engines."

Now that I thought about it, I remembered that the trains that used to go through the tunnels in Hemphill billowed white smoke as they emerged from the openings in the mountains. Now, they just emerged from the tunnels near our house with a loud chugging sound.

Since the train was so slow in passing, Dad remarked, "Your Grandfather Tom Bromfield used to jump on trains when he was a boy before he started working in the mines at the age of twelve. He and some buddies used to throw his little brother up into a moving boxcar, and quickly jump into the boxcar and ride the train to Williamson. Then, they would ride the train back home and throw his five year old brother off and jump off the train again."

We listened and waited for what seemed like twenty minutes, watching as the Tuscan red passenger cars slowly passed us. I was sure that we would be late for the movie, but finally the last car passed the crossing gates. It had a round glass observation car; so we waved, as we always did when a train passed.

To save time, Dad stopped right past the tracks and turned into the Welch Municipal Parking Building, which was the first municipal parking building built in the United States. He navigated the dark, narrow concrete ramp, and pulled into a spot on the second floor. We walked back down the ramp and up McDowell Street just a few steps to the Pocahontas Theater.

We approached the glass booth, and Dad told the young lady that he wanted an adult ticket and two children's tickets. As I stared at the small octagonal marble tiles that covered the entry, he handed her a dollar bill and waited for his change and the three paper tickets.

Dad pulled open the heavy wood and glass doors with large brass rails for handles, and we entered into a magnificent and ornate world. I was at first bombarded by the delicious smell of rich, hot buttery popcorn as I walked past a large window displaying the latest fashions available at The Beryl Shop, located next door to the theater. There was one of those same glass cubes with cascading liquid, like those at the bus station, but this one had red liquid flowing down the inside of the glass. Dad stopped at the brightly lit counter and asked if we wanted some popcorn. John asked for the new space drink, a green liquid served in a plastic replica of a Mercury Space Capsule, like the one Alan Shepherd had just ridden into outer space. I just asked for a box of Sugar Babies, as I admired the beautiful rich colored carpet and large movie posters.

We started into the darkened theater, and John and I noticed a sign that pointed up and said, "Balcony Seats Fifteen Cents". John asked Dad if we could go sit in the balcony, and he answered, "That's for the colored people. We can't sit there."

As my eyes adjusted to the darkness, I saw right in front of us, a dark polished wooden wall separated the lower section and the upper section. Behind the upper section was the balcony, which I could not see at all in the darkness. I noticed the plush carpet continued from the lobby into the theater and up to the stage with the huge white screen, flanked by burgundy velvet curtains. On the walls in fancy plaster alcoves were ornate lights, which were dimmed until they were switched off when the movie started. We chose seats on the first row of the upper section. The closer we got to our chosen seats, the stickier the carpet felt. The soft seats folded down, and they had a distinctive dusty smell put there by years of entertainment seekers.

As we were seated, the screen lit up, and we saw previews of coming attractions and two Bugs Bunny cartoons. Then the movie started. It was "Gorgo", a thrilling black and white monster movie. I thought it was terrifying to watch Gorgo destroying towns and homes until his mother (a much bigger monster) showed up at the end of the movie. She was really huge and scary. She took her son Gorgo back into the sea with her, and all was well, except for the people who were killed or homeless in the destroyed towns.

As we left the theater, the sharp March wind scratched at my legs beneath the dress I wore. It had been an exciting birthday for John. In the car I asked him how he liked his space drink. He said it was "nasty", and that he would never get one of those again, if we ever got another chance to go to the movies.

I thought about how in just the past year I had seen the passing of steam engines and the advent of space travel. President Kennedy had said that America would put a man on the moon by the end of the 1960's. The 1960's would certainly see many changes, if indeed an American could land on the moon.

The frosty March wind made the clothes dance on the line in the sunshine, especially the dark brown support hose that Mom wore to help her varicose veins. They had cost twelve dollars a pair, (that was a LOT of money for Mom and Dad to spend.) But, the doctor had prescribed them for relief from the ache in her legs. Then, one day, when I came home from school, Mom was crying. I was really scared because I had never seen her cry before. When I asked her what was wrong, she said that when she hung her stockings on the clothes line to dry, the neighbor's bulldogs had seen them "dancing". They began to bite and claw the stockings until they were in shreds.

When Mom went to get the support hose from the line, they were in tatters on the ground beneath the clothes line. Mom was upset because she had no others, and she knew that we could not afford to buy any more. For the next few months, she wrapped her aching legs in beige Ace bandages when she needed relief from pain.

A next door neighbor and Mom developed a rapport based on mutual need. Mrs. Henderson could sew, and Mom was not really good at it. So, Mattie Henderson would "peg" my brother Ron's pants for him. She would make the pants legs narrow at the ankles. Mom would perform little deeds for Mattie in exchange, like bake a lemon pie for her. One day, when I got home from school, there was a large bookcase with a drop down desk and drawers in the entry hall. It was beautiful with its ornate scrolling and the glass door. I quickly found Mom cooking pinto beans in the kitchen. "Where did you get that bookcase I asked?"

"It's a secretary," Mom answered as she smashed a bean against the side of the pot to check for doneness. "It's an antique, and I traded Mrs. Henderson a raincoat for it. I already cleaned it up, polished it, and put books in the cabinet. Doesn't it look good in the hall?"

I had to agree, and I spent the rest of the afternoon exploring the pigeon holes and drawers in the desk. When Dad came home and saw it, of course, he asked Mom where she got it. When she told him of the trade, he became irate.

"All right," he said, "but the next time it rains, since you don't have a raincoat, just put that thing on your back and go on out in the rain." That was the second time I saw Mom cry.

Operetta costume-"Colored Camp" is in the background

CHAPTER 10

"Spring has sprung;
The grass has ris';
I wonder where
The flowers is."

With the first spatters of white on the dark hillsides we knew the "sarvis" trees were in bloom and that spring was on the way. Dad always said that "sarvis" blossoms made the best honey, but we didn't care about that. We knew it was time for the kids to get outside and ride their Christmas bikes up and down Spruce Street for another few months. The first bikes always prompted Mom to tell about Uncle Buddy as a boy.

One day Buddy brought half of a bike home. His dad asked him, "Boy, where did you get those bike parts?"

"I found them on the riverbank," he replied.

The next day Buddy brought home additional bike parts, obviously belonging with the first parts.

"Boy, where did you get those bike parts?" asked his father.

"I found them on the riverbank," again he replied.

Of course his father knew that Buddy had stolen a bike and disassembled it to disguise this fact, but he let him keep the bike. He knew that he could never afford to buy a bike for his son. He could hardly feed them during those depression years. After that, whenever anyone in the family had something that they did not want to reveal where it came from, they always said, "I found it on the riverbank."

In early spring before the undergrowth in the woods became thick, Dad brought home sassafrass roots that he had dug up. He opened his lunch kit and among the waxed papers that had wrapped his sandwich and the snowball cake wrapper were small reddish roots. Mom washed them carefully, put them in a pot with water and boiled them to make sassafrass tea. Each family member was obliged to drink some because Dad said it was a good "spring tonic". Its root beer, herbal flavor (sort of like Teaberry gum) was not bad, especially if a little sugar was added to the cup. We truly believed that the sassafrass tea was "good for what ails you".

It always seemed that springtime was when "tummy aches" would surface. If I told Mom that my stomach was hurting, her first question was, "When was the last time you went to the bathroom?" If I answered any day but today, she would say, "I probably need to wash your bowels out." That meant that the red rubber hot water bottle was filled with warm water, and an enema was administered in the bathroom. It was the most dreaded treatment; so I soon learned not to complain of tummy aches, unless they were really serious.

Springtime was the season when we could finally get outside and rediscover our Hemphill world, always remembering the rules: never touch the guide wires on the telephone poles because you could get shocked, never throw rocks in the river because you could "pitch over" into the river and drown, never eat green apples, or you will get a tummy ache, and never take things that don't belong to you. This last rule was the one that John broke every spring because it was time to play "marbles". He and his friends would draw a ring in a patch of dirt. Each boy put the same number of glass marbles in the middle of the ring, and they took turns "shooting" a special marble into the circle and trying to knock as many marbles as possible out of the circle. The shooter kept all of the marbles that he knocked out, whether they were his or not. This was thrilling to the boys because it was a form of gambling that was sanctioned by mothers throughout Hemphill. The boys even drew a ring with a piece of sandstone on the paved school playground and played during recess at school. Mom even made John a special marble bag by cutting off blue jeans and sewing the leftover leg on one end and inserting a leather string in the top to make a drawstring. This was very sturdy for carrying John's winnings to and from school. John even walked across the river to "Leonard Young Stadium" to shoot marbles in the black dirt beside the railroad tracks, if the bigger boys were not playing ball there.

"Leonard Young Stadium" was what my family called the wide spot between the mountain and the railroad tracks and the river near Uncle Buddy's house. It was called that because it was the only semi-level spot in Hemphill big enough for the boys to gather and play games of football or baseball. It was called "Leonard Young Stadium" because Leonard Young owned one of the few footballs in Hemphill; so no one could play unless Leonard was there. And, if Leonard happened to get mad about how a game was going at the time, he took his football and went home. Therefore, the wide spot was aptly dubbed "Leonard Young Stadium."

The problem with "Leonard Young Stadium" was that it was only a narrow strip of dirt, made black by the dust and droppings from coal trains that long ago had stopped using the tracks. If a ball was thrown or hit too far, it could not be caught because catchers would have to run into the road or over the railroad tracks. Footballs thrown or kicked too far to one side would end up in the murky waters of Tug River, causing the boys to form a sort of "leap frog" brigade of rock throwers along the river bank. Each boy would take a station along the bank of the river and throw rocks at the floating football to try to force it toward the bank. Then the next boy would do the same while the first boy would move down the river to throw a stone again. When the football came close to the bank, one boy would reach or wade into the river and retrieve the ball. In the spring, this could take several hundred yards, or even miles, to retrieve the precious football, and usually at times like these Leonard would take his worn brown football and go home.

    Baseballs, on the other hand were more expendable. If a baseball was thrown or batted into the river, the boys would just get an old sock and wrap it with black cloth friction tape. They would immediately have a new ball just like the lost one. We never knew where the friction tape came from, but everybody had a roll at their homes. It must have been "supplied" by the coal companies and brought home in miners' dinner buckets.

    Spring was the season when teachers asked to fill a slotted card with dimes for the "March of Dimes". The money was to be used to fight polio. Polio was a crippling disease that we were constantly warned about, even though we had received the new vaccine in the late 1950's. We were warned not to play on the river bank, or you'll catch polio and end up with leg braces or in an iron lung. My friend Debbie's father walked with crutches because he'd had polio in his younger days. So, John and I dutifully begged for dimes to fill our cards, and then we received a plastic crutch pin to wear.

      Springtime at Welch Elementary School was the time of year that we always planned, practiced, and presented an "operetta". This was an elaborate performance with music, dancing, and costumes. Each class had a part in the program. In second grade, I had been a crepe paper adorned flower that blossomed after the girls dressed as raindrops with shredded plastic laundry bags sprinkled me. This year, I was to perform the "patty-cake polka", dressed as a little German girl. Mom had to ask Mrs. Henderson next door to make the required cotton red jumper and white apron, and she gladly sewed the rick-rack until it was perfect. We practiced many times in the school music room and on the school stage. My partner was Roy Kliner, and I secretly thought he was very cute, though he was no Bobby Gray (the coolest kid in my class.)

      On the night of the operetta, we danced beautifully as we sang "Brother, come and dance with me; both my hands I give to thee." The entire program went off without a hitch—

almost. The sixth graders were the last class to perform. They were dressed as Caribbean Islanders singing "Day-O", a song about working on a banana plantation. At the end of the song, they "tossed" (actually threw) bananas into the audience. A firm banana hit Mom right between the eyes. Luckily, it did not break her glasses. Mr. Brown, the principal, and several teachers rushed to check on her, but she assured them that she was fine. Because our act was finished and I was waiting back in the classroom, I did not see all the commotion.

However, the next day all of the kids at school were talking about the woman who got hit in the face with a banana. I never told them that it was my mother.

While we had operettas every year at Welch Elementary School, the students at Welch High School put on a "May Court" every May. Spring days after school were spent practicing dances, such as a "May Pole Dance" or a routine with a popular song at the time like "Purple People Eater". These acts were performed by underclassmen for the seniors who were chosen by the student body to be on the May Court. There was a May Queen, who wore a white formal gown and a May King, who wore a tuxedo, complete with tails. There were three May Princesses, who wore formal gowns of pastel colors, and three May Princes, who wore tuxedoes without tails. Finally, there were twenty members of the May Court. The senior girls wore formal gowns, usually with a large hoop underneath, like Southern belles, and the boys wore white dinner jackets.

In 1961, my sister Janice was on the Welch High School May Court. She wore a pale blue strapless gown with layer upon layer of ruffles, and in the back was a bustle. It was breath-taking when she was introduced as "Lady Janice Gaye" of the "House of Vandell", as "Pomp and Circumstance" blared in the background. She stood with all of the other members of the court in a semi-circle on the gym floor for the two hours it took for the performance. After all, the performance was, theoretically, in their honor, but I think the audience enjoyed the acts more than the May Court did.

Warmer weather brought plowing and planting time. Dad loved to dig up the dirt on the hillside above the house and plant onions and lettuce when the "signs were right", according to the Farmer's Almanac. As the ground got warmer, he would plant green beans, tomatoes, and squash. He always spent spring evenings after work and Saturdays doing his beloved planting. This spring, however, was different. I noticed more and more that Dad was home when I arrived home from school and already busy plowing and planting in the garden. It seemed that he only went to work two or three days a week now. I overheard Mom asking why he wasn't working tomorrow, and his reply was that the coal company did not have many orders for the coal; so he was not needed to supervise the day shift tomorrow. He added, "At least I work all of the days they need me, not like Lenny Hurt back before the War."

One spring day right after sunup Lenny and his buddies were walking to work at the mine in Shaft Bottom. They decided that it was a perfect day to "lay out of work" and go fishing or just loaf around the company store. So, Lenny said, "I tell you what. I will throw my dinner bucket up the air, and if comes back down, we will go back home and not work today. Lenny threw the shiny tin bucket, loaded with sandwiches, pie, and extra drinking water, high into the air. In fact, he threw it so high that it lodged in the branches of a locust tree, with leaves that were just beginning to sprout. The buddies were amazed. The lunch bucket had not come back down; so that meant that they would have to go to work that day. However, they were not to be thwarted in their plan to "play hooky" from work; so they began to throw rocks at the bucket to try to dislodge it from the branches of the tall, rough-barked tree. Finally, one of the miners walked the short distance to his house, got a long pole, hit the branches repeatedly, and got the dinner bucket to fall to the ground. After all of that effort, the miners turned around and went back home, rather than spending that perfect spring day miles underground in the dark, damp mine.

Spring was the season for new life, and as the birds built nests and began to lay eggs, new kittens or puppies would arrive at homes on Spruce Street and be added to the already fairly large menagerie of coal camp pets. One of the most loved (by kids) and most hated (by adults) pets on Spruce Street was T. J. T. J. belonged to Jerry, who lived two houses up the street. T. J. was a very large light brown sheepdog who looked just like the star of the Disney movie "The Shaggy Dog". Although T. J. was large and friendly, his fur was always dirty and matted because he ran around the neighborhood freely, getting into mud puddles, coal piles, and even the sewage-filled Tug River. He would run among the freshly washed sheets hanging out to dry, or chew the cushions on porch chairs left out overnight. This made him the enemy of most adults on Spruce Street, but his flopping tongue and wagging tail told the kids that he was their friend.

    One day when I walked home from the bus stop, I noticed that T.J. was conspicuously absent on the street. I began to ask everyone, "Where is T. J.?"

    Even Jerry, who hardly ever knew where T. J. was, except at feeding time, was worried. Finally, when I asked Mom, she said, "I saw the dog catcher come this morning. He was driving a white panel truck. He tried to coax T. J. into the back of the truck, but T. J. would have nothing to do with that. A few minutes later, I saw the dog catcher driving up the street with T. J. in the passenger's seat, sitting up with his tongue hanging out. T. J. looked like he was happy to be going for a ride in the truck. Little did he know, he was probably never coming back".

When Dad came home from work that day and Mom told him that story, he laughed and said, "You are just like T. J. You get in the car and sit up and ride, not always knowing where you will end up."

They both laughed, knowing that Dad was referring to the fact that Mom did not drive and depended on Dad to take her where she needed or wanted to go. It didn't really matter that Mom did not drive because we only had one car anyway, and Dad had to take it to work each day.

Very soon after T. J. disappeared, I came home from school to find a different car parked in the wide space across from the house. (Dad had criss-crossed railroad ties on the river bank and filled the structure in with dirt to make a parking space across the narrow street from our house.) The shiny pink and black Dodge had been parked there this morning, and now there was a hideous two-toned green Plymouth in its place. The car was old, and it looked like a grasshopper hunched over, ready to spring. As I rushed in the door, I asked Mom whose car that was in our parking spot. Mom was writing a check for the fourth quarter of Ron's college tuition. She answered in a serious tone, "Your Dad traded for it today."

"Where did he get it?" I asked.

"Pickleseimer's Used Cars", she answered. I couldn't believe it. Why would anyone willingly exchange the pretty new Dodge for that ugly old green thing?

Just then, the phone rang. I ran to the desk in the front hall and picked up the heavy black receiver. It was fairly new with a dial, with our new number HE6-2206 in the center. (The "HE" stood for "Hemlock".) The phone before it had been black also, but when I picked up that heavy receiver attached to a straight cord, an operator always said, "Number please." Our number on that phone had been 105L. Also, that phone was on a party line, and we sometimes had to wait for Lily Neil to finish her conversation before we could make a call.

As I answered the new-fangled phone, my cousin Connie's voice was excited on the other end, "Randy Cochran got saved!"

"What are you talking about?" I asked in disbelief.

Connie continued with an animated tone. "Randy Cochran got saved last night at the tent revival!"

I had seen the large canvas tent in the wide space near Dr. Anderson's office at the end of "colored camp." In years past the space had been the location of Welch Coal Sales; so the area was covered with black coal dirt. Before the tent was erected, the workers diligently covered the soot-covered lot with five or six inches of sawdust. Then the tent was put up. When the tent sides were tied up, we could see rows of wooden folding chairs and electric lights strung up in the front where a podium stood. At night we could hear the melodious rise and fall of the preacher's voice on a loudspeaker, although we could not hear the exact words he said.

Now, Connie was telling me that the most notorious resident of Hemphill—the former reform school pupil had gotten "saved" at this tent revival. I had heard that God could work miracles, and I had even heard about miracles in my own family, like John's miraculous healing when he was a baby. But this was more incredible than I could fathom. Randy Cochran was a criminal. How could he be saved to "sin no more?"

"How do you know about this?" I asked Connie.

"Everybody's talking about it," she said. The people who were there said he went to the front of the tent when the preacher gave the invitation as the congregation sang 'Just as I Am.' When the preacher prayed for Randy, he started to cry and shout. They said the 'Spirit of the Lord took holt of 'im.' Then he laid down in the floor and began to roll around. He got sawdust in his hair and all over his clothes, but he didn't care because he was 'in the Spirit.' It's a miracle!"

It was a miracle, all right. It was the opposite of what I expected, and I was terrified that other changes might be on the way.

CHAPTER 11

May, 1961, was a time of change throughout the land. My older sister Janice, after being on the May Court, graduated from Welch High School and immediately left for Myrtle Beach, South Carolina, with the Senior Sigma Sorority. They had raised money all year and enjoyed a week at the Harmony House Motel, just as all senior members of the sorority had done each year. I couldn't wait until I was in high school so I could be a member of the "Sigs". Upon her return from the beach, we were all greeted with a surprise announcement from Mom.

"We are moving," she said matter-of-factly. "Uncle Buddy and Aunt Anna Belle have agreed to trade houses with us," she continued.

I was shocked, even horrified, to think of moving into that four room house with a dirt front yard and *an outhouse.* Why would Mom and Dad want to leave our large, white, four-bedroom house for a faded gray four-room house, with no bathroom?

Mom kept talking in an even tone. "This house cost $3,500 when we bought it four years ago from Mr. Swope, and we still owe him quite a bit for the house. (Mr. Swope bought several houses when the coal companies sold them to the public. Then, he resold them for a profit.) Buddy and Anna Belle's house is paid for. So we are going to trade them even. They will take over the payments on this house, and we will not have a house payment after the trade. That way, we can still afford Ron's college tuition and all of the other expenses we have."

I was disappointed and scared. "How will we fit all of our things into four rooms?" I asked timidly.

"We will have to leave some things in this house. After all, Buddy and Anna Belle only have four rooms of furniture to fill this ten room house," she replied.

"What about taking baths and using the bathroom?" I asked.

"When I was growing up, we took a bath in a big round metal washtub, and we used an outhouse. We can do the same until your dad gets a bathroom built onto the house," she answered.

Well, at least there was hope. Dad was planning to build a bathroom onto the house. It couldn't be soon enough for me.

Mom continued, "At least we are only moving a short distance, not like your Uncle Donnie who had to move his family all the way to Oregon to find a job after he was "cut off" (laid off) at the Trailee Mine."

I thought about that for a moment. Many coal miners from Hemphill and other coal camps had recently been laid off and forced to move to a big city to find a job. Some of our relatives and friends had moved to Detroit (pronounced DEE-troit in Hemphill) to find work in the factories.

Some had moved to Cleveland and Cincinnati. They now lived in apartments, and the kids played on city streets or in parks. I had heard how my cousin had been mocked at school for her "hillbilly" accent. I thought about all of that and decided it might be better than moving into the house that we were heading for.

On moving day at the beginning of June, Nester's Transfer Company from North Welch dispatched two trucks to Hemphill, one for our belongings, and one to move Buddy and Anna Belle's family and belongings into our house. It was a bit chaotic, since each family's belongings had to be moved out before the other's things could be moved in, but, at least the distance was only a mile or so.

When the movers arrived and started dismantling beds and moving the couch and chairs, it soon became apparent how many of our belongings were to be left in the house on Spruce Street. We left the beautiful mahogany desk in the entry hall, the small pool table in Ron's bedroom, the dining room suite, and everything that was stored in the attic. We couldn't take the built-in breakfast booth, so Anna Belle left her black iron kitchen chairs with a gray formica topped table. She wouldn't need it anyway, with our breakfast nook and the dining room furniture.

"Good morning, Miz Vandell," the large friendly mover named Charlie said with a grin. "Remember the last time we moved you folks to another house in Hemphill?"

Mom and Dad were moving to one of the ten or more houses they had occupied in Hemphill. Since Mom had just had a baby recently, her sister Tootsie was there to help with the move.

At that time, Mom and Dad had two washing machines. When they got an automatic washer, the wringer-type Maytag was moved onto the porch. They also had two couches and two refrigerators for the same reason. The movers commented to each other, "Gee, this man has two of everything. He even has two women!"

Mom smiled at Charlie and said, "Yes, I remember very well."

Finally most our furniture was on the large orange truck and I looked one last time at "our" house on Spruce Street. I walked through the empty living room, my footsteps echoing on the oak floors, with no rugs or curtains to absorb the sound. I looked at the brick fireplace and thought of stockings hanging on the mantle at Christmas. Where would we hang our stockings in the new house, without a fireplace?

We walked one last time up the street, around the curve, down the stone church steps, by the playground, past the post office, across the swinging bridge next to Quattrone's Grocery Store, and up a red dog (burned refuse from a slate dump) covered road to our new home. It didn't even have a street address, and I was so ashamed to call it "home".

After the moving men had left and we began to straighten and put away things and make the beds, I began to feel even more confused and ashamed of our new circumstances. We did have the beautiful antique secretary that Mom had traded her raincoat for, and, of course, the mahogany upright piano fit in the small alcove in the living room. Janice could still play hymns on it for us. Other than those niceties, most of the things we brought were bare essentials. As I carefully explored our new dwelling, I noticed two small holes, neatly patched, on the wall in the room that John, Janice, and I were forced to share. John whispered that they looked like bullet holes. I was getting worried about this new "neighborhood", if it could be called that; so I asked Mom what the holes were. She said she wasn't sure, but that this was the house where Anna Belle's father, Ol' Man Persinger, had been shot during a heated poker game, but that had happened on the front porch. Now, I was not just ashamed and worried, I was purely scared to live in this house that had seen gambling, murder, and other unknown violence.

When "nature called", I slowly made my way up the makeshift stone steps to the gray unpainted outhouse. As I turned the small piece of wood than spun on a nail and served as a lock, an acrid odor overwhelmed me. It was raw, unadulterated urine and feces, and I gagged as I entered. This outhouse was a "one-holer". It had only one hole with a hinged wooden lid. I lifted the lid, and the stench became even stronger. I quickly released the pent-up liquid into the hole, hearing the urine sort of "thud" into the area beneath, not the usual splashing against water that I had heard in the white porcelain toilet in the house on Spruce Street. As I looked for the toilet tissue, I noticed that it was on a coat hanger that was hanging on a nail. It was sort of damp from being "outside", but it seemed clean; so I used it, and dropped it into the black smelly hole. I was trying to hold my breath the whole time to keep from inhaling the noxious fumes, but as I closed the wooden lid, I glanced down into the hole, just to be sure that I did not see any BB guns in the toilet. Many times Mom had told stories about her brothers' misadventures with BB guns. One time Buddy shot a bird with his new BB gun, and their father threw the gun into the toilet. Another time, their grandfather said to her brother Buddy, "I bet you can't shoot that lion in that picture on the wall." Buddy immediately shot the lion, and that BB gun ended up in the toilet too. I was just curious to see how many BB guns were in this outhouse, but I didn't look close or long enough to spy any.

    Late in the afternoon, with the beds made and supper on the stove, the phone rang. It was Uncle Buddy, calling his old number. He wanted to know if we would move back into the house on Spruce Street. They wanted to trade back. He would pay for both of the moving vans, if we would move back. Buddy said that Anna Belle was unhappy and that the kids already missed their friends.

 Friends??? What friends? The only kids I had seen all day were Rod and his brother Junior, who lived up on the hill. Rod had showed me his half a forefinger. Rod said that Junior was holding an axe, and Rod laid his finger on a tree stump and said, "Junior, I dare you to cut my finger off." Immediately, Junior cut the finger off with the ax. Surely, these were not the friends that my cousins missed so much. Besides, they had MY friends on Spruce Street to play with now, and my friends had *all* of their fingers, and their toes, too.

 Mom calmly assured her brother Buddy that everything would be okay. She said that she would talk to Dad when he came home from work, but that we should not do anything hasty. Maybe we should give Anna Belle and the kids time to get adjusted.

 Inside, my heart was leaping, hoping against hope that we would move back to the sanctuary of Spruce Street. As a few days passed and Buddy's family adjusted to my house and my friends, it became apparent that we were staying in the four-room unpainted dwelling. We would be using that disgusting outhouse on the hill and taking a bath in that round galvanized tin "number 3" washtub.

 It took great effort to fill the tub and bathe; so, we did not bathe every night. We just "washed up" some nights, and hair washing was out of the question, except on Saturdays, when there was more time.

    First, Mom put down newspapers (the Welch Daily News) on the pine floor of the kids' shared bedroom. Then she put towels over the paper and brought in a large tub in. Next she ran hot water from the kitchen sink into buckets, carried the buckets into the bedroom, and emptied them into the tub until it was about one-third full. Mom bathed first, then Janice, then I bathed, and lastly John, since he usually the dirtiest from playing outside with his friends—all in the same water. Then, the REAL work began—emptying the dirty water from the tub. The metal bucket was filled with the gray bathwater and carried to the back porch and thrown over the railing. This took several trips because clean water was added as each bather entered the tub. By the time the tub was almost empty, the thin metal handle of the bucket had left marks on my hands. The last bit of water was carried in the tub to the back porch, hoisted over the railing and dumped into the back yard. A bucket of clean water was used to rinse the soap scum and dirty residue from the tub before it was hung on a nail on the back porch. Then, the towels and newspaper were picked up, and the whole family was clean. I was just glad that Dad showered after work every day at the coal mine because his coal dirt covered body would get the water REALLY dirty.

    As the summer progressed I began to take long walks up the dirt road that led to the top of the mountain. From the top, I could look down on the town of Welch. I could see the backs of the stores on McDowell Street (Murphy's and Cox's Department Stores and the Flat Iron Drugstore.) I remembered the story Dad told about bringing mules up McDowell Street in the 1930's. I could visualize the scene as I looked at the town below.

Dad was a young employee of the Semmet-Solvay Coal Company in Hemphill. They still used mules to pull the coal cars in and out of the mines on railroad tracks. So, one day Dad was sent across the mountain to Tazewell, Virginia, to get some mules that the coal company had purchased from a farmer there. Dad and Lenny Hurt were driven in a company truck to Tazewell and dropped off at the farm. They were to bring five mules back across the mountain to the mine in Hemphill.

Dad and Lenny each rode a mule and led the other three on narrow rutted dirt roads over the steep mountain, down Gary Hollow, and through the mining community of Havaco. By the time they reached the Riverside Drive area of Welch, they were tired and "saddle sore," and a mist had started to fall, eventually soaking them.

They led those mules on the paved street (which is U. S. Route 52) and proceeded to go up the one-way Wyoming Street in Welch that would lead them to rest in Hemphill. However, the streets at that time were paved with bricks, and the misty rain had made them very slippery for the mules. As Dad and Lenny tried to get the mules to go up the hill, the stubborn creatures slipped and fell several times on the brick streets, and at last, they refused to go at all.

Dad had a real problem, but he realized that McDowell Street (the other one-way street through Welch) was level because it followed the river, which occupied the narrow strip of level ground between two steep mountains. So, Dad left Lenny with the mules, went to the Welch police station, and asked the police chief to stop traffic on McDowell Street so that he could get the mules through town. The chief laughed at such a problem, but he finally agreed to stop the traffic on both ends of the level one-way street. Dad and Lenny then coaxed the mules to go back down to McDowell Street, and they led those mules through Welch just like a parade, with pedestrians stopping to watch the spectacle. Dad had found a solution to a difficult problem, and he and Lenny delivered the mules safely to the Hemphill mine.

On the way back home on the steep, rutted road that led down the mountain, I found several locust shells, or husks. I realized that this must be the year of the locusts that invaded every seventeen years. I thought of the irony of the locust invasion, and tears filled my eyes. I felt as if my whole life had been invaded by locusts and that everything down to the bare bones had been destroyed. Then, I realized that Dad had found a way to solve his problem with the mules. Maybe he could find a way to get us back to Spruce Street. I prayed very hard every day.

John on the steps of Uncle Buddy's house - after renovations   Tearing down the outhouse

CHAPTER 12

The first Monday morning arrived in our new house, and Dad and Mom got up at 5:30, as usual, so that Dad could get ready to go to the mine for the day shift. As she had done since 1935, Mom stood at the stove frying bacon, while at the same time, wrapping a sandwich for the dinner bucket in waxed paper. Suddenly, a knock on the back door startled her. She cautiously opened the door, and there stood an unkempt man who lived high on the hill in a tumble-down house. As she stared at him, he said, "Excuse me, Ma'am, but I am Sam Bordy. I live up on the hill, and I have been watching for your kitchen light to come on. You see, I work for the city (of Welch), and I need to be at work at seven o'clock, but I don't have a clock. Could you tell me what time it is?"

Mom, a little confused, told him that it was 5:40. He thanked her and went back up on the hill toward his house. After that morning, Mr. Bordy knocked on our kitchen door every "workday" to gage the time that he should be leaving for work. Then, one day, the knocks ceased. Although we never asked, we assumed that Sam had finally gone to G. C. Murphy's and bought a clock.

    The summer of 1961 was a frenzied time. Chubby Checker was still making it big with "the devil's music", as Mom called it, and the world was "jerking" and "twisting" all summer long. In Hemphill, we were in a different kind of frenzy. Almost from the first week of the move, Dad was engaged in some sort of home improvement project. First, Danny Craft and his cute nephew Wilson from up Warwick holler, began to build in the old back porch to add a bedroom and a bathroom to the house. It took several weeks because a cesspool had to be hand dug and lined with cinder blocks, but finally, it was done. The bathroom fixtures were not new, but there was a white cast-iron tub set on four by four blocks of lumber because the claw feet were missing. More importantly, there was a sparkling white commode; so the outhouse was out of commission, although it still stood like a sentry up on the hill.

    Next, my brother Ron and a college friend spent many days painting the peeling gray house a fresh white. Meanwhile Dad spent evenings and Saturdays building rock walls and planting grass to create a real yard, and building sturdy stone steps and walkways. He also made a parking spot beside the "red dog" road, rather than in the front yard. Everyone was in a frenzy it seemed, except me. I spent that summer feeling isolated and watching 1930's movies about Broadway and eating popcorn and cookies and, of course, walking up on the hill and looking at the city of Welch, wondering why I couldn't live on a regular street like the other kids in my class.

One day when I my lower lip was particularly droopy, Dad said, "Your lip is hanging down so low, you could make shoe laces out of it."

I whined, "I miss my friends on Spruce Street."

Well, that didn't set well with Dad, since he was working so hard on the new house. He replied matter of factly, "Look at you. Cryin' with a loaf of bread under your arm."

I really didn't know what bread had to do with me and my sadness, and if the remark was meant to make me count my blessings, it really didn't work.

On the other hand, John stayed connected to his Spruce Street friends, going there to play every day. One day he came home wearing strange clothes and carrying his wet and smelly clothes in a bag. "Whose clothes are you wearing?" Mom asked.

"These are (Cousin) Willard's clothes. Anna Belle let me wear them home because my clothes got wet," John answered.

Of course, Mom asked how his clothes got wet and he told us about riding "car tops" in Tug River. Some of the bigger boys would use an ax to chop the roof off of abandoned junk cars found along every back road in Hemphill. They would drag these "car tops" down to the river, turn them upside down, and ride them like a raft. They would stand in them and guide them with a long board or pole. It seemed that John and Willard had "acquired" a "car top" from some boys. As they were guiding down the middle of the river, it tipped a little and began to fill with water. Quickly, they found themselves standing in the middle of the polluted Tug River with the "car top" beneath them on the river bottom. Luckily, the river was only about two feet deep that summer; so they walked to the shore and to our old house on Spruce Street to get cleaned up and dried off.

    Although nobody in his right mind would intentionally go swimming in Tug River, John spent many days on Spruce Street swimming in Hemphill's first "in-ground swimming pool." The Burkes family had moved into the house at the end of Spruce Street. Mr. Burkes created a swimming pool by first acquiring an old dump truck and removing the bed of the truck that was used for hauling coal. He dug a hole in the yard big enough for the truck bed and placed it in the hole. When filled with water from a hose connected to the fire hydrant on the hill. (Since he worked for the city of Welch, Mr. Burkes had a special wrench for the hydrant.) The actual truck bed was the pool, and the part of the bed that had been over the cab of the truck was the deck for entering and exiting the pool. The "deck" made a noise when kids walked on it or dove from it, but otherwise, it was the perfect summertime refresher.

    The last week of June and the first week of July were set aside for "Miners' Vacation." Every year the coal mines stopped production for two weeks to allow employees time off. In years past we had gone to Boone Lake in Tennessee or to visit relatives, but this year, there would be no trip. Dad needed the time (and money) to work on our new house.
    During the two weeks of Miners' Vacation, it seemed strange to see grown men standing on the streets of Welch, talking and waiting for their wives, who were spending the extra "vacation pay" at J. C. Penney's or Murphy's Department Store in Welch. We knew they were miners because their eyes were encircled with dark outlines like mascara or eyeliner marks. No matter how hard these men tried, the coal dirt stayed around the sensitive eye area and in their pores, leaving an unmistakable black "ring around the collar."
    During his vacation that year, Dad worked all day, building rock walls around the house. He meticulously stacked the shaped stones to create a smooth wall that would help make a terrace, or level area, on the hillside. In the cool evenings he rested on the front porch in his same green metal bouncing chair. As I sat in the green painted rocker next to him, he grinned and said, "There goes some

miner in his 'Vacation Special.' You can tell it's a 'Vacation Special' by all of the blue smoke coming out of the tail pipe."

A "Vacation Special" was a used car advertised in the Welch Daily News. The price was calculated to be just the amount of a miner's vacation pay (a few hundred dollars).

Dad continued, "Last year, Junior Pickett bought a 'Vacation Special' to take to Alabama to visit his wife's family. He said it burned nine quarts of oil on the way; so he left it in Alabama, and he and his wife rode the bus home. Those 'Vacation Specials' are special, all right."

Even though John returned to Spruce Street every day, I was reluctant to go back. I felt that I no longer belonged there—that I had been replaced by my cousin Connie and her family. Connie, however, kept in touch with me regularly, often calling me on the phone to chat. (We kept our same phone number: HE6-2206.) One hot day Connie called and suggested that we go climb the slate dump that was in "Warwick Holler", near our house. I really did not know what that involved, but I was bored with watching the carpenters and watching those 1930's "Broadway" movies.

When Connie arrived, she carried a bag of magazines. "What is in the bag?" I asked.

"Shh," she whispered. "They are *True Romance* and *True Story Magazines.* Don't let your Mom know that I have them."

We told Mom where we were going, and we headed up the rutted dirt road that led upward into Warwick "Holler." We passed unpainted houses similar to our four-room abode with junk cars (Hudson was emblazed on the side of one) and old tires in the yards. Smelly gray "wash water" ran from pipes near the houses into ditches along the road, and green flies and "skeeters" buzzed all around the gray foul-smelling water. Along the way, we admired wildflowers like Queen Anne's lace and stopped to pick a few ripe blackberries. Finally, we came to the pond, a small body of water covered with yellowish green slime we called "stagnate". The pond had been formed when the slate refuse from the mine in Warwick "Holler" had been dumped there and blocked a mountain stream. Rising above the pond was the massive slate dump that we had passed on the way to the mountain top cemetery where my grandmother was buried. It was as tall as the mountain, and it was mostly black, but years of time had allowed a few hearty trees and bushes to take root among the hard gray stones.

With Connie carrying her bag of magazines, we began to climb the black mountain. It was not really hard because the slate moved slightly with each step, forming a foothold, or step, for climbing. The real problem came if the slate moved toward the bottom of the hill too far or too quickly. After several minutes and a lot of sweat, we reached a plateau and sat down to rest. Connie pulled her magazines out of the bag. We sat all afternoon and read them. I had never read such stories because Mom would not allow "racy" magazines or books in our house. I was titillated and enthralled by the "real" romantic escapades of the characters. When we had had enough of the "literary" experience, it was time to go back down the slate dump. We stood up and started to step down the hill, finding that the slate gave way with each step, producing a sliding sensation. We slid down, down, down easily, stopping to empty our shoes of the black pebbles and dust that accumulated in them. (I had worn slip-on shoes that were easy to remove, but became ruined by the black, ground-in dust and dirt.) When we got to the bottom, we found ourselves laughing so hard that we could hardly talk. When we could finally speak, we decided to climb up and slide down again. We repeated the climb four times, until we were too hot, tired, and dirty to climb again.

    As we walked home with our feet (and bottoms) filthy, we talked about our now mutual friends on Spruce Street. Then, we decided that we would climb the slate dump again, and we did many times in the weeks that followed. We were always careful not to injure ourselves on the slate dump because once the coal dirt got into a wound, it would stay there, even after the cut or scrape healed, leaving a "coalfield tattoo". These black or gray colored designs marked my knees and the knees of most of the kids and adults in Hemphill.

Besides climbing slate dumps, that summer held another exciting activity—picking blackberries. The delicate sweet berries grew right beside many of the dirt roads near our house, and when they were ripe, we took aluminum "kettles" and small galvanized tin buckets to the berry patch.

As we left the house with our containers one Saturday morning, Dad said, "Don't forget to take a stick with you."

I asked, "Why do we need a stick?" "To beat the bushes and drive away the snakes," he answered. "If you don't scare the snakes away, they will think your hand is a bird when you reach between the branches for the berries. And, they will bite you before you know it."

Well, that took some of the enthusiasm out of the expedition, but we dutifully found a long thick stick and used it to move branches and check for snakes before reaching back into thickets for the berries.

When John, Janice, and I had filled our containers, we walked the short distance on the "red dog" covered road back to the house. Mom quickly washed them and began to make a blackberry cobbler and blackberry preserves. We would have the cobbler that evening with supper, and the preserves would remind us of our blackberry picking times every time we sampled some on cold winter mornings.

During blackberry season, there were often knocks at the back door, and boys would ask timidly if Mom wanted to buy a gallon of berries for fifty cents. She always bought the containers of delicious fruit and froze it for cobblers and jams to be made later on. In our new house we had a large chest-type freezer that Uncle Buddy had bought at the Trailee Company Store. When they had moved, they had left it in the kitchen because it was too heavy to move (they said); so Mom filled it with berries and vegetables every summer.

    As the days of summer lost their appeal and became boring and dusty, I began to feel the normal yearnings for school to start again. Things had changed that summer, but many things stayed steadfastly the same. I still walked to Quattrone's Grocery Store and to the post office for Mom. They were even closer than they had been when we lived on Spruce Street. The major difference in running errands for Mom now was the dreaded swinging bridge. It was a "pedestrian structure" that connected our section of Hemphill near Warwick "Holler" to the main road through Hemphill where the stores, post office, and playground were located. You had to cross the swinging bridge to get to the school bus stop too. The bridge consisted of a rough board walkway with gaps that allowed a full view of the murky water below. The boards were suspended from two thick wire cables that were attached to concrete pillars at each end of the bridge. When people walked across the bridge, their natural gaits would cause the bridge to swing. That was scary enough, but many times bored older boys would watch for kids to cross the bridge. They would pounce on the bridge and jump furiously, causing the bridge to bounce up and down wildly, like ocean waves. The older boys thought it great fun to terrify unsuspecting kids, especially as they crossed the bridge on the way home from the school bus stop. I viewed the bridge as a dreaded obstacle, and I always tried to check for boys lurking around the bridge before I crossed.

    The end of summer in America is traditionally considered to be Labor Day. Labor Day, 1961, also heralded the end of the outhouse. Dad tore it down, board by board, and filled in the foul-smelling hole. The removal of the outhouse was a time of celebration. Its demise seemed to symbolize that our new house was now a "regular" home, albeit, not like the ten room house we had left, but a clean, safe home, still the same.

    After that summer of 1961, I returned to Welch Elementary School in the fall. It still looked the same, and I was still in the same class with most of the kids from the year before. However, some of them did not seem to recognize me. Surely moving had not changed my appearance, but, in essence, it had. The summer spent watching TV movies and eating popcorn had left its mark on my figure. (I should have known that when the neighbor started calling me "Chubby".) It seems that even my beloved fourth grade teacher Mrs. Santoro did not even recognize me at first, but as the first days of school passed, things became normal again, almost.

The most abnormal thing about school in fifth grade was my teacher, Mrs. Trainer. She was a tall, thin, gangly woman with a shrill nasal voice. Her pinned-up dark hair gave the appearance of a witch-like prison matron. She seemed to be obsessed with the fact that Leif Erickson, not Christopher Columbus, discovered America, and she asked that question on every social studies test during the entire year. Mrs. Trainer had a pencil with a wooden football on the eraser end. She had probably bought it from the Welch High School Pep Club. She walked between the rows of desks and hit students on the head if they were not paying attention as she thought they should. At lunch, she used a spoon to smack the hands of errant students. These smacks were always accompanied by whiny nasal reprimands. One day, after reprimanding Jimmy several times, she asked him, "What would your father say about how you are acting?"

He looked at Mrs. Trainer unashamedly and said, "He'd say that you are nuts!"

We all tried to stifle our snickers, but we really admired Jimmy for his honesty. We all thought that Jimmy would get a paddling for sassing. Occasionally, teachers ordered disobedient or disrespectful students into the hall. After asking for a witness from a teacher in a nearby classroom, we heard "whack,

whack, whack" echoing throughout the hallway. Then, the errant student returned to his desk, usually very subdued and penitent. But this time, for whatever reason, there was no paddling for Jimmy. That was the thing about Mrs. Trainer—she was so unpredictable. For sure, Mrs. Trainer was no Mrs. Santoro, and we truly felt that she *was* nuts.

    As time passed, even though I never liked our new house, I came to see that not much had really changed. Our family was still in Hemphill. Dad was still working, five days most weeks. And, Dad still drove us to the First Church of God on Stewart Street, even if it was in the ugly green bug-like car. One Sunday morning in October, as I looked at the stained glass window at the front of the church, the words of the song that I was singing, pricked at my heart and my mind. I realized that the words from "It is Well with My Soul" might be one key to my happiness. "Whatever my lot, Thou hast taught me to say, 'It is well with my soul'." At that point I realized that even though I could not have a real street address and I could never again live on Spruce Street, my life was still virtually the same. With my parents' loving upbringing, I would be all right, as long as I "remember my raisin' ."

EPILOGUE

Changes in our lives came continually throughout the decade of the sixties, and we intently watched most of those changes on our new color television. We sat spellbound as announcers counted down and manned rockets flew into space, eventually landing men on the moon in 1969. The changes that continued to come throughout the 1960's (everything from mini-skirts to "free love" to the Viet Nam War to integration and the Civil Rights Movement to the Beatles to food stamps) impacted lives in Hemphill, as in the rest of the nation. (However, things tended to reach Hemphill a little later than other places. We were always a little behind the times, except in the area of welfare. McDowell County was the FIRST part of the United States to use food stamps.) Even through an era of unimaginable innovations in music, fashion, technology, and moral values, our family remained a steadfast constant in our lives. Our make-do self sufficiency, with a dependence on the Almighty, kept us firmly rooted through good times and "hard times".

The Vandell family lived in the small house for five years, constantly painting, building, and improving the house. In 1966 we moved next door to a larger, nicer house, where we lived when my sister Janice worked at the Social Security Office in Welch and got married to a fellow employee. Always seeking a better home, my parents moved again into one of Hemphill's few brick houses in 1975. Things got better and better for the family. The "hard times" seemed to be gone.

My brothers and sisters have continued to live and raise families in the manner that was instilled into their lives in Hemphill. My brother John graduated from college and lives in Bastian, Virginia. He has retired as an inspector for the State of Virginia.

I went to college and became a teacher, always striving to become a master teacher like Mrs. Santoro. I got married, and my husband and I have two adult children. We live on a real street with a real address, and we even have indoor plumbing. Yet, no experience has had an impact on my life like the years I spent in Hemphill. I cherish those times, and I hope I will always "remember my raisin'".

APPENDIX:
RELATED RECIPES FOR A TASTE OF COAL CAMP LIFE

Blackberry Cobbler

1 stick margarine
1 cup self-rising flour
3 cups blackberries or other fruit (heated)
1 cup sugar
1 cup milk

Preheat oven to 350 or 375 degrees. Melt margarine in 9"x13" pan as the oven preheats. In a separate bowl, mix flour, sugar and milk, and stir until smooth. Pour over melted margarine. Do not stir!!! Spoon warm fruit on top and bake 45-50 minutes until brown. Serve with whipped cream.

Christmas Party Punch

Mix:
2 cups double strength tea
2 Party-Pak* Ginger Ale
1 Party-Pak Strawberry Soda
1 Party-Pak Orange Soda
½ gal. orange sherbet
1 pk. frozen strawberries
¼ c. Realemon

*A Party-Pak is approximately 1 liter.

Pickled Eggs

3 cups white vinegar
2 cups beet juice
1 ½ cups sugar
1 tbsp. salt
6-8 whole cloves
6 black peppercorns
1 cinnamon stick

    Put ingredients in a pot. Heat to boiling and simmer 15-20 min.

    Peel hard boiled eggs and put into large glass jar (1 gal.). Remove cinnamon, cloves and peppercorns from liquid and pour hot liquid over the eggs in the jar. When cool, refrigerate until pickled (at least one week).

Popcorn Balls

1 Tbsp. butter
1 cup sugar
1 cup molasses
1 Tbsp. salt
4 quarts popped corn

Melt butter and add sugar, salt, and molasses. Boil to the hard-crack stage (285 degrees). Pour mixture over popped corn and stir while pouring. Rub butter on your hands and shape the mixture into balls while it is warm. Be careful; it will be hot at first. Wrap balls in waxed paper. Do not refrigerate.

Rhubarb Strawberry Pie

1½ cups sugar
2 Tbsp. quick cooking tapioca
¼ tsp. salt
¼ tsp. nutmeg
3 cups rhubarb, cut into ½ in. pieces
1 cup sliced fresh strawberries
1 pie crust and enough dough to form a lattice
1 Tbsp. butter
In a large bowl combine sugar, tapioca, salt, and nutmeg. Add rhubarb and strawberries and mix well to coat fruit. Let stand about 20 min. Spoon fruit mixture into pastry lined 9" pie plate. Dot with the butter. Moisten the edge of the pastry. Top with slices of pastry to form a lattice and flute the edges. Bake at 400 degrees for 35-40 min. If desired, decorate the lattice top with sliced fresh strawberries dipped in melted currant jelly.

Snow Cream

1 tall glass of new-fallen (not yellow) snow
Evaporated milk, a.k.a., Carnation Canned Cream
1 Tbsp. sugar
2 drops vanilla
Fill glass with clean snow. Pour in a little milk. Add sugar and vanilla. Stir and enjoy!

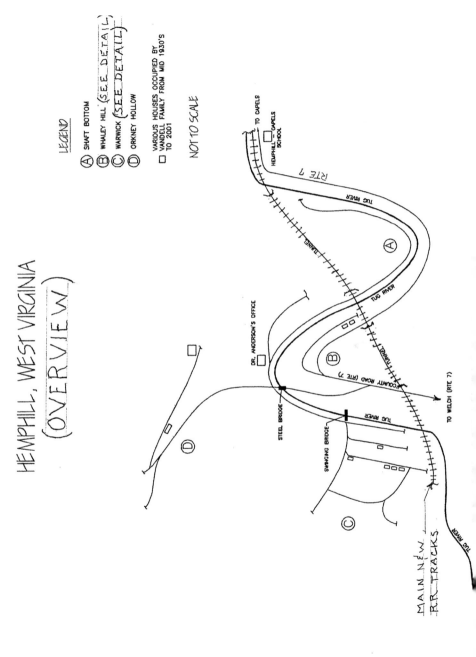

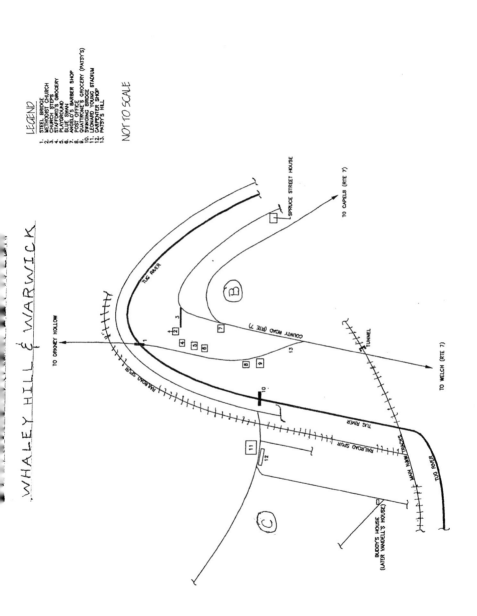